11th International Conference on E-Learning in the Workplace (ICELW 2018)

New York, New York, USA
13 – 15 June 2018

Editor:

David Guralnick

ISBN: 978-0-9827670-8-5

Printed from e-media with permission by:

Curran Associates, Inc.
57 Morehouse Lane
Red Hook, NY 12571

Some format issues inherent in the e-media version may also appear in this print version.

Printed by Curran Associates, Inc. (2018)

For permission requests, please contact Kaleidoscope Learning
at the address below.

Kaleidoscope Learning
41 Madison Avenue
31st Floor
New York, NY 10010
USA

Phone: +1 212 679-2740 or +1 800-693-5950

info@kaleidolearning.com

Additional copies of this publication are available from:

Curran Associates, Inc.
57 Morehouse Lane
Red Hook, NY 12571 USA
Phone: 845-758-0400
Fax: 845-758-2633
Email: curran@proceedings.com
Web: www.proceedings.com

TABLE OF CONTENTS

The Bank of Georgia Learning Hub

Tina Balavadze[1], Tatia Zhgenti[1]
[1] Bank of Georgia, Human Capital Management Department, Tbilisi, Georgia

Abstract

The purpose of this project is to offer Bank of Georgia employees a unique ecosystem of resources, inspiration and collaboration, as well as opportunities to increase the positive impact of work. Joining a diverse community of people will inspire, connect, and enable employees to develop their best work potential every step of the way. The goal is to develop a smart space to live the "learning" as a corporate value and promote learning as a constant process to help each other evolve and push the team toward improvement in their professional paths. Main principles: no formality, more informal relations, openness and genuine interest.

Index terms - **Moodle; learning culture; experience sharing; open source; transformative learning;**

I. Introduction

The goal of the new learning concept was to recreate the learning experience for over 5000 employees, for the learning process to become a pleasant routine for self-development for the front office as well as the back office, suitable for both directions in order to master position-related requirements and have resources to acknowledge the latest updates on general working skills, motivation, leadership and self-awareness.

"Developing a learning culture is no longer just another fanciful idea. It is becoming more imperative for companies to cultivate learning if they wish to stay in business".[1] Despite this trend, in Georgia you rarely see organizations driven by learning culture, especially one oriented on transformative[2] learning.

Bank of Georgia managed to position itself as the market leader and one of the largest employers in the country. Rapid growth was originally very important in terms of competition, but once the position was established, the need to create something of value for internal users became apparent. Because nothing is more important for the development of an organization than employees who are satisfied and have development opportunities, we set the following goal:

Develop a knowledge and experience-sharing platform within the organization that would promote personal and professional development and growth.

In order to achieve this goal, a few milestones had to be marked and reached: a) Transformation of F2F learning experience; b) Development and promotion of eLearning culture; c) Sharing the future – building the cross-functional teams for knowledge and experience sharing.

II. Importance and Transformation

While development and promotion of learning culture within the organization, for both employers and employees, is quite common in Western culture, the reality of post-Soviet Georgia is entirely different: if you know something - you have more responsibilities; if you are the only one with specific knowledge within the company – you are irreplaceable; if you can get promoted anyway, why would you share knowledge, or help others? These are common stances in many Georgian organizations. Therefore, creation of the learning programs direction by the human capital management department under the slogan "helping each other to succeed" was a quite unexpected and bold statement.

Either people would go along with it and we would succeed, or all our work would remain just a bit of "fun" had by back office employees. We began taking classic change management steps[3] in order to change the mindset among employees, increase employee satisfaction and decrease turnover in the long run; we believed all this would allow us to achieve increased efficiency, productivity and profit and that each employee taking part in the knowledge and experience sharing process would feel ownership and accountability for the accomplishments of the organization;

The first step taken in order to implement not just learning, but transformative learning culture, was to clearly demonstrate the necessity for change to decision-makers; it was as if they all felt something needed to change, but no one knew exactly what this "something" was; on one hand, a business knows well the results it needs to achieve and how many people it needs to achieve them, but stopping to think about how to get there is rare, as there is simply no time to do it. However, it is critical in a modern competitive environment to know what skills, and not what knowledge a person in a specific position should possess. Everyone gladly answered our questions. Our task was to figure out how to help employees achieve their full potential.

After an in-depth analysis, we created a kind of cross-functional "coalition", identified problems and determined the main challenges and opportunities, arriving to what the optimal solution would be:

[1] Creating a Learning Culture for the Improvement of your Organization April 7, 2015Tala A. Nabong https://goo.gl/CaUa2K
[2] Mezirow, 1991
[3] John P. Kotter

Challenges & opportunities	**Solution**
Career paths & horizontal development – front office employees cannot see prospects for horizontal development, they do not know what to do, what knowledge or skills are needed to move to a different position on the same level;	Direction routes need to be created and requirements for each position should be made visible; what to read, what to work on in order to be selected;
Leadership pipeline – BoG offers quite a few programs for talents, but by means of sending employees emails and asking them to reply if they are interested, which causes a lack of transparency and a feeling of injustice – why was someone else selected and not me?	An open registration system for courses
Knowledge hoarding	Collecting reflective experience to promote experience sharing
Knowledge acquired during trainings is subject to frequent change, and employees have a hard time associating separate events using logic, as they tend instead to memorize each piece of information independently from one another.	Switch from knowledge-based learning model to skill-based (where applicable)
What we call trainings are really lectures and training an employee (a teller, for instance) requires a very long time.	Quick provision of various targeted information; Decrease of F2F training hours; Creation of a micro-environment which will allow employees to keep up with change and implement it.
Banking processes and procedures frequently change and updating employees about these changes only with informational letters is not effective.	Provide information on changes otherwise than only in writing (which may be difficult to process)
Up to 3000 employees are required to attend several trainings per year, for which the organization needs to have them travel to Tbilisi.	Webinars, online tutorials, tracking training attendance;

The next step was to put together a team that would be able to develop a strategic vision and an initiative package as for what, how and when things needed to be changed and achieved; and all this needed to be prepared so as to ultimately build a positive attitude to learning among employees.

III. Developing Transformative Learning Culture

For developing and supporting this idea, we decided to use a Moodle-based Learning Management System (LMS) as a knowledge-sharing platform to promote experience sharing. In our case, using an open-source solution had several distinct advantages:

- This was not just implementation of eLearning, we were tackling the challenge of implementing transformative and digital learning at the same time;
- This was a cheap and painless solution for a project with a high risk of falling through.
- We did not know how more than 5000 employees would respond to this package of changes: F2F trainings in a new format, switching to digital for a large part of technical trainings.
- To be honest, the entire process was learning by doing for us in the first place.

A) Transformation of the learning process; What brought this change on?

In this modern information world where people need to acquire various competences in order to achieve professional development and successful careers, it becomes more and more important not only to accumulate knowledge, but also to be able to process, categorize, analyze it, use it as needed etc.

- This is especially important for the newly hired employees who attend trainings as the initial stage of starting their job.
- Until now, trainings were given in a lecture-type format and were not really in line with new developments in the education field. Participants had a hard time memorizing information presented by the trainer and transferring it into practice without personal involvement and active participation.

B) Teaching methodology; What changes took place?

The teaching methodology is based on modern teaching-learning principles, which include active involvement of the participants in the training process and developing of key competences for the profession.

The following activities were offered to the participants: a) Processing and analyzing information using various strategies; b) Reviewing realistic situations and role-play using effective communication; c) Discussing open, reasoning questions; d) Preparing presentations about products and introducing them according to a sales plan; e) Joint processing of different issues and focusing on teamwork; f) Sharing the acquired experience etc.

The role of the trainer has evolved, it is now more of a guiding person who uses specific instructions and reflective questions to encourage the participants to comprehend and discuss in depth the topics envisaged in the program. By creating various practical, realistic situations, the trainer also helps the participants getting acquainted in advance with the environment they will be working in.

C) Teaching format

The trainings format is currently mixed; in addition to face to face trainings, there is now the learning.bog.ge distance teaching module. Participants spend part of the learning process working independently in the system.

This was made possible by creating: a) Texts and assignments for distance learning format; b) Video instructions for Core banking software; c) Digital Assignments; d) An online testing database.

Distance assignments allow:

- Focusing more during the training process on the importance and advantages of each product and ways to offer them;
- Participants to take more responsibility for their learning, to gain understanding, analyze, ask themselves questions (what have I grasped well, which parts are still unclear to me, etc.) and review them with the trainer on the next day;
- Developing digital literacy in participants;
- Saving time for the trainer, who can then use it to monitor the participants' progress and for personal professional development.

D) *Integrated topics*

Before the introduction of renewed programs, participants took part in separate trainings about topics, service standards and sales components relevant to their position. This approach made it difficult for the participants to put together and in practice information collected at different times from various trainings.

In order for the participants to perceive activities carried out in the frame of their position as a whole system and be able to transfer them into practice more easily, the renewed programs integrated service standards and sales components.

- Service standards are distributed throughout the training days and there is a constant focus on them;
- After each product has been covered, participants present them using the sales plan;
- Products are offered using service standards during rolc-play.

E) *Material*

- Long sentences that made it difficult to assimilate information have been divided into shorter sentences;
- The material has been adapted so as to be in line with research results on how many new words people can memorize and understand in a given context on one occasion.
- Texts have been edited, grammatical errors and sentence structuring have been corrected.

F) *Evaluation system*

The change in training methodology, allowing the participants to collect knowledge, develop skills and outlooks, clearly required a renewed evaluation system as well.

- Evaluation became multi-sided, with everyone responsible for the training taking part (participants, trainers, instructor, future monitor);
- Reliable and valid criteria for evaluation of the participants were developed based on the program goals and challenges;
- Achievement level features were described in detail in the assessment criteria;
- Assessment criteria and forms are known in advance to everyone interested.

The trainer and the instructor assess participants based on criteria known in advance to everyone and not on personal views and test scores. In addition to the score, they put in writing constructive feedback that is oriented on professional development of the participant.

A questionnaire was also created for assessment of the trainer and instructor by the participant, to measure their professional competence and their teaching skills.

Participant

The participant continuously receives feedback, which helps in self-evaluation and identification of one's own strong suits and areas for improvement. The participants are also involved in the process of refining the training, as they fill out reflection cards several times, focusing on topics they tackled successfully as well as the challenging parts, to which the trainer will then return.

IV. Moodle customization;

Our choice fell on Moodle to be developed as a learning platform for Bank of Georgia employees. The project started in August with a 3-month timeline. On November 15th, we were ready to launch a system configured, developed and redesigned to match our needs and the employees' expectations.

The most valuable experience was the understanding that the system is for users, and while making every decision on configuration or any other issue our metric was to revisit the solution from an employee's perspective. Having restricted time and budget, this meant tradeoffs. Although the system is not really the best possible option from administration user experience perspective, it still is considered as great learning platform, which was a goal we kept in mind throughout the project.

In terms of the length of the process, considering the challenges and the involvement of the internal team: the trainers, the content managers and the system team practically achieved the impossible: a) Adaptation to requirements of a modern organization; b) Collecting reflective experience;

From the beginning we've been thinking about LMS as a platform to run and manage all learning & development related processes. Implementation process of LMS as we perceived it would require a lot of time and financial resources. And actually it would drive us away from the main goal we have stated above. So we concentrated on creating a platform for knowledge and experience-sharing within the organization that would promote personal and professional development and growth.

In our understanding this was a platform where we could create and/or input diverse content with outstanding user experience. Which could give more than basic analytics on Employee interests, engagement and their learning outcomes. The Team's prior experience with LMS gave a hint that Moodle could have been the most cost effective alternative if having a knowledgeable implementation team.

The main difficulty was to find a vendor who had good experience in implementing Moodle as Enterprise LMS, which is an absolutely different from Educational Organization. And it is worth mentioning that the project was considered by Company as fully outsourced solution with internal product owner, thus practically no support was provided by internal IT team.

Georgian Software Implementation Market can be characterized as scarce, and even scarce when we are talking about Moodle. We found a vendor, with fairly good recommendations. Although the working process can be named as mismatch of expectations based on first impressions. The challenges can be summarized as: a) No outline for communication throughout the project; b) Wrong expectations for requirements gathering, documentation preparation/delivery and UAT cycles, that was triggered by our experience of having either internal development projects, with mostly waterfall principles or acquiring SAAS solutions, which is leveraging the functionality the way it is, without heavy configurational changes, if any. c) Mindset change for whole team:

- Changing the course content format and structure for Content team, which was an enormous work including: acquiring the skills necessary to go through this process and fulfilling this huge work.
- Acquiring new knowledge and skills for System Administration team and input Moodle driven changes into a daily routine seamlessly.
- Game changing experience for trainers, to perceive Moodle as their Supportive Mechanism and not a Competitor.
- Accepting the reality of becoming a main system support and developing group for a technical team, which means listening to system users, trainers, content managers, system administrators, translating their needs into technical solutions, researching the available options and discussing them with broader team, before making a final decision on solution and implementing it.

These challenges required some set of skills, beliefs and circumstances which made this project a reality:

- The environment of learning by doing
- Flexibility
- Perceiving failure as a learning opportunity and having courage to start all over again each and every time.
- Great support from the Vendor in terms of Consultancy with content structuring and creation.
- Our firm belief in a positive outcome of a Project.

As a result, we had the pilot version of the project launched in November and the project Go Live after a 3-month pilot period.

V. Results

Just a few weeks after full scale live launch of the Moodle based learning management system, we are seeing: new forms of learning for professional/position related skills and knowledge enhancement: video materials, instructions and tutorials; Structured and adapted (simplified) reading, procedures and manuals; self-check exercises that allow the participants to understand that evaluation is not a punishment measure, that the main thing is to work on one's self and skill improvement and we will provide them with material in various formats so that they can assimilate it more easily, depending on what type of learner they are; the teaching process, entirely conducted via LMS, is as follows:

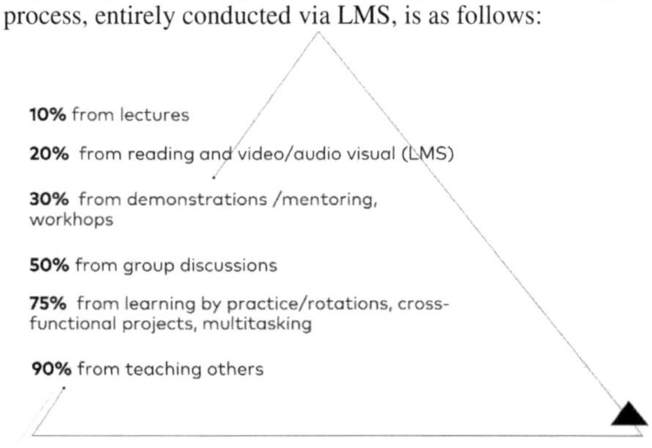

- publications (HBR / Leaders Digest/ New York Times) translated into Georgian;
- A space where you can not only learn, but also teach and become the media for learning to colleagues – any employee who considers they have the ability to teach something interesting to colleagues, whether it's project management, Excel formulas, effective email writing or other, is helped by our team in preparing a well-structured curriculum for a training; using LMS, employees register for this F2F (and later also for eCourses); with this approach, the motivation of tutor employees is very high and more and more employees wish to be involved in this process;
- Fancy interface and thought-out user experience: an attractive main page displaying headlines on every learning, training and various activities; various course structures including course content, allowing employees to select the programs they wish to be involved in; Easy and intuitive navigation, which made it easy to adapt to the new platform; Idea and experience-sharing within blogs and forums; ultimately, it is another internal communication tool that brings colleagues even closer together;
- Reporting is very important for any company; Moodle allows installing plug-ins that give very valuable analysis regarding each employee. It is possible to have grade books, which on one hand will motivate employees, and on the other hand show managers clearly the employees' progress and direction of development. Participants give detailed

feedback for each program, allowing continuous improvement of the trainings.

- Needless to say, implementation of eLearning turned out to be very effective for conducting time-consuming trainings and significantly decreased traveling and printing expenses;
- Flexible platform to evolve with company and employee development needs. As an open source platform with probably the largest and most active community, various plug-ins will guarantee the most up-to-date enhancements to the learning process and content management.

VI. Conclusion

We believe the Learning Programs slogan "helping each other to succeed" can be considered precisely chosen. As a result, we strive for a reality of increased efficiency, productivity and profit, where each employee takes part in the knowledge and experience sharing process and feels ownership and accountability for the organization's accomplishments. The first steps forward this goal can definitely be considered encouraging:

- Identifying challenges & solutions together with main stakeholders;
- Building up a team with capability to achieve the goal with positive attitude in employees;
- Implement digital tool to support the change;

We consider it to be a successful start of the exploration journey to find the best solutions to support the learning experience at Bank of Georgia. We have positive feedback from learners and their managers as a visible improvement in skills' application after the training being reported. We strive to create an environment of sharing and learning to promote and support the culture of self-development.

References

[1] Mezirow, Jack. (1991). Transformative Dimensions of Adult Learning.

[2] Biech (editor) (2017) ASTD Handbook: The Definitive Reference for Training & Development 2nd Edition.

[3] Holman, Devane, Cady (2007) The Change Handbook: Group Methods for Shaping the Future.

[4] Dirken Design For How People Learn (Voices That Matter) 1st Edition.

[5] John P. Kotter Leading Change, 2012.

Authors

Tina Balavadze – Learning Programs Director, Human Capital Management Department, Bank of Georgia (e-mail: t.balavadze@bog.ge).

Tatia Zhgenti – Head of Platforms Development Unit, Human Capital Management Department, Bank of Georgia (e-mail: tzhgenti@bog.ge).

3D Modeling and Simulation of Airflow and Aerosol Deposition of Idealized Human Oral Airways

Abdurrahman Addokhi[1], Abdullah Albedah[1], Omar Altwijri[1]
[1]Biomedical Technology, King Saud University, Riyadh

New drug delivery methods require the drug to be delivered to a specific region with the right dose. Inhalation is a primary drug delivery method. Details on the aerosol deposition in the human airway are needed for studying the causes of some airway diseases and designing new drug delivery systems via inhalation. In this study, three different models of the human upper respiratory tract (URT) differing in their simplicity were modeled. The 1st model had no tracheobronchial (TB) airways, the 2nd had symmetric TB airways, & the 3rd had asymmetric TB airways. After doing an airflow simulation on all three models, it was found that the 1st model will not be reliable for aerosol deposition simulation. A multiphase simulation was done on the 3rd model which consisted of air and water particles to study the effect of flow rate and water particle diameter on the deposition of water particles in the URT. The multiphase simulation showed that the particle deposition in the URT increases with the increasing of the flow rate and the particle diameter. The results of this study agreed with previous experimental and numerical studies of the aerosol deposition in the human URT.

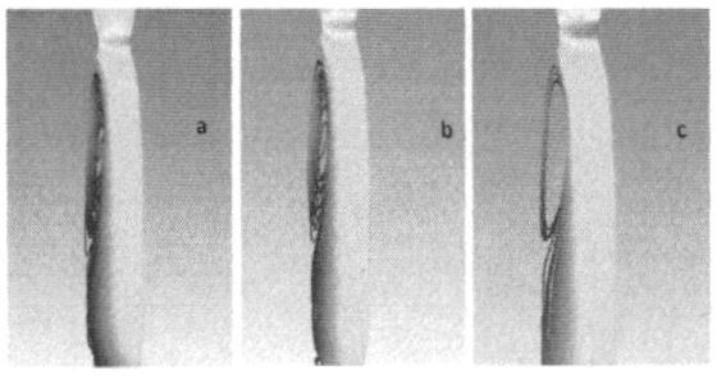

Figures 2.2.2 a,b, & c Closer look to the recirculation zones of the three models.

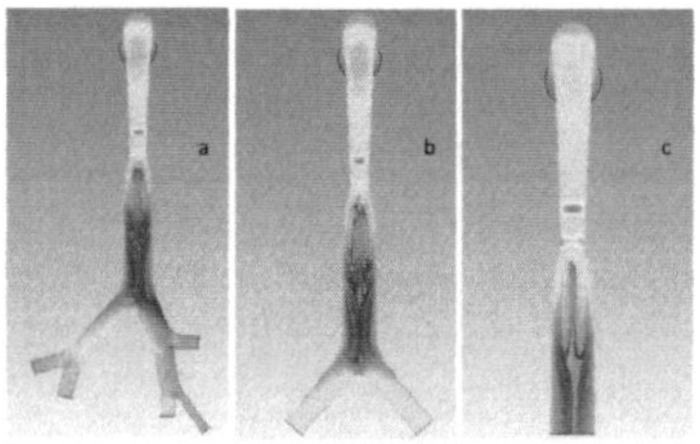

Figures 2.2.3 a,b, & c Back side view of the stream lines of the three models.

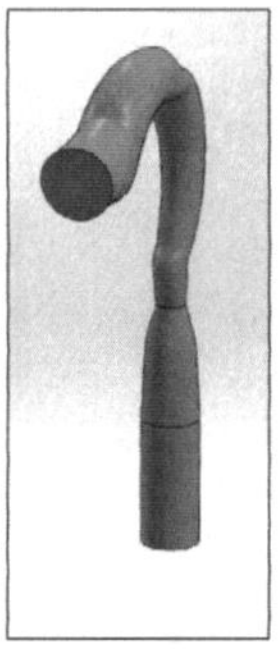

Figure 2.1.2aURT model without a TB airway.

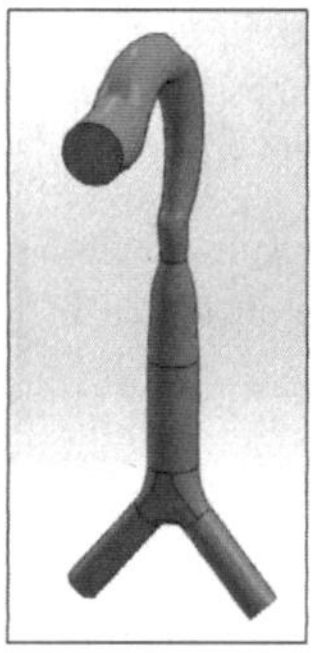

Figure 2.1.2bURT model with symmetric TB airways.

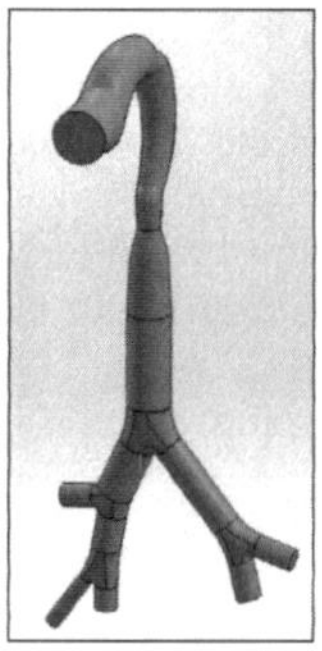

Figure 2.1.2cURT model with asymmetric TB airways.

Understanding Users of Adaptable E-Learning as Heterogeneous Groups of Work-Integrated Learners

Amir Haj-Bolouri[1] and Lars Svensson[1]
[1] University West, Trollhättan, Sweden

Abstract— **The increasing adoption and use of E-Learning at workplaces outside of academia, create challenges and problems for the future of designing sufficient E-Learning solutions. Workplaces are challenged on daily basis by the constant implications of digitalization in society. In turn, practitioners need to adapt toward the implications and learn new technologies that are aligned with their practice. Their practice however, varies due to factors such as, workplace culture, professional roles, areas of responsibilities, etc. This makes it difficult for workplaces to adopt traditional E-Learning solutions that are configured for traditional E-Learning users such as, students and teachers in academia. As an attempt to discuss such problem, this paper problematizes users of E-Learning at workplaces outside of academia, as practitioners that are heterogeneous. Subsequently, this paper introduces learning outcomes from a research case, where the concept of Adaptable E-Learning was incorporated. Additionally, the contribution of this paper emphasizes users of Adaptable E-Learning as heterogeneous groups of work-integrated learners. Work-integrated learning is thus incorporated to problematize the aspect of heterogeneity and to advocate adaptable E-Learning solutions that integrate theory with practice.**

Index Terms—**Adaptable E-Learning, Work-Integrated Learning, Users, Heterogeneous**

I. INTRODUCTION

E-Learning is understood as pedagogy empowered by technology that involves learning through interaction with digital artifacts (e.g. computers, smart-devices), which are connected to a network, giving people the opportunity to learn at almost anytime, anywhere [1-2]. Universities in particular, have a prolonged history of adopting and using E-Learning to provide distance learning environments (e.g. MOOC's) for students and teachers. The past two decades have seen extensive changes in higher education in terms of increased access to education, lifelong learning, increased choice in areas of courses, and the personalization of learning [3-4]. Additionally, workplaces in the industry (outside the context of higher education) have adopted E-Learning to help practitioners acquire necessary skills and knowledge for their work [5]. And due to large variety of workplace characteristics - with respect to culture, practitioners, professional roles, etc. – the need of adopting supportive E-Learning at work, increases efficiently over time.

Consequently, workplaces face challenges with determining how to adopt E-Learning successfully [6]. Such challenges include: whether adopting traditional E-Learning is successful or not [7]; strategizing flexible E-Learning methods and techniques that are adaptable toward situated needs and requirements [8-9]; bridging pedagogical and theory-based guidelines for flexible design of E-Learning at work [10]. Another problematic issue concern practitioners' individual abilities of learning how to use E-Learning technologies for their work, sufficiently. This issue is affected by practitioners' heterogeneity in terms of their age, background, culture, language, professional roles, education, knowledge expertise, and overall worldview (e.g. beliefs, norms, values). Different practitioners are thus in need of different learning styles that are adaptable toward their heterogeneous needs and requirements.

In this paper, we will address the issue of practitioners' heterogeneity, by problematizing their roles as users from a work-integrated learning perspective [11-14]. More specifically, we will introduce the concept of *adaptable E-Learning* as a response by arguing that: (1) E-Learning at work needs to be adaptable in order to successfully address practitioners' heterogeneous needs and requirements; (2) subsequent workplace culture needs to enable learning at work through participation and embodiment of practitioners' work experiences, continuously; and (3) learning tasks need to be integrated with practitioners' work activities, rather than be presented as detached learning objects. In order to incorporate our arguments, we will present learning outcomes from a case where adaptable E-Learning was introduced to support heterogeneous groups of practitioners. Based on the learning outcomes, we understand such practitioners as heterogeneous groups of work-integrated learners.

The remainder of this paper is structured as follows. Section 2 discusses related work on users of E-Learning at work and work-integrated learning. Subsequently, section 3 introduces learning outcomes from a case of adaptable E-Learning. Finally, section 4 concludes the paper.

II. RELATED WORK

A. *Users of E-Learning at Work*

Since more than a decade, the subject of E-Learning at work has become an interesting topic for researchers (see, e.g., [15-18]). The use of E-Learning at work has enabled workplaces to support their practitioners in developing skills, competencies, and knowledge. Positive motivators of using E-Learning at work include factors such as, ease of accessibility (e.g. online-tutorials); cost-effectiveness; delivery-efficiency; self-directed learning; and flexibility in time and place [19-20]. However, users of E-Learning at work do also experience negative associations with using traditional E-Learning at work. Such associations include, that it is impersonal; too framed and stiff; frustrating; lonely; time-wastage (easily distracted); unreliable; and poor quality or too gimmicky learning programs [21].

According to Freund [21], individual needs of E-Learning users at work, are difficult to address sufficiently. Their needs vary heavily due to the variation of them as individuals, and the variation of their domain of work (e.g. practice, roles, expertise). Thus, traditionally E-Learning solutions are experienced as restricted, lack of personalization, lack of collaboration and interactivity, as well as not learner-oriented toward the heterogeneity of users [10] [21].

Their needs of developing new skills, competencies, and knowledge, are thus not equivalent to the needs of traditional E-Learning users such as students of higher education. Rather, their needs are heterogeneous and explicitly directed toward their domain of work (rather than a formal education). As an implication, scholars (e.g. [10] [15] [21]) argue and call for alternative thinking that help understanding users of E-Learning at work, their heterogeneous needs, and how future E-Learning solutions can address them.

B. *Work-Integrated Learning*

One major challenge of incorporating users of E-Learning at work, is how to integrate their personal development of skills and knowledge, with competencies that are sufficiently relevant for their work. This create tensions for how to pedagogically structure E-Learning environments, and how to enable online support through the learning process [10].

From a broader perspective of learning at work however, this tension is directed toward socio-cultural ideas of work-integrated learning. This include theories of learning as situated within communities of practice in learning [22-23]; the emphasis on supporting practitioners' reflection in practice [24-25]; a dual continuity of integrated work and learning activities [11-14]; and learning activities that are intuitively embedded in everyday practices [26].

Consequently, traditional E-Learning solutions tend to reduce the capacity of adapting toward these different modes of work-integrated learning, and are thus experienced as detached (both form and content) from practitioners' everyday practice. Additionally, the heterogeneity of practitioners affects the tension and have an effect on the conditions and processes of which work-integrated learning is supported through. For these reasons, scholars (e.g. [10] [27]) have indicated that: different modes of work-integrated learning need to incorporate research knowledge from various sources, which help understanding the complexity of learning at work. This is argued to be important for providing adaptable E-learning solutions. We will therefore adopt a work-integrated learning perspective that we find especially useful from the viewpoint of incorporating a case of adaptable E-Learning.

III. A Case of Adaptable E-Learning

A. *Empirical Setting*

The empirical setting of our case was organized and executed within a municipality in the West region of Sweden. The municipality is responsible for supporting the integration work of newly arrived immigrants in Sweden (also known as, *newcomers*), through a supportive program that incorporates newcomers' civic orientation. The purpose of the civic orientation program is to inform newcomers fundamental phenomena of society such as, democracy, laws and regulations, and everyday practicalities of living in Swedish society.

Originally, the program was provided through 60 hours of classroom teachings, divided into different sessions for different groups of newcomers (e.g. from Somalia, Syria, etc.). However, due to the highly intense arrival of newcomers in Sweden, the municipality decided to support the program (between 2013-2016) by introducing E-Learning solutions that help providing civic orientation sessions to a larger throughput of newcomers in Sweden – for more detailed information about the case and prior research outcomes, please address the references [27-30].

A crucial objective of the case was to support the practitioners of civic orientation (known as *integration workers*) through E-Learning solutions. The integration workers are practitioners that have different roles and areas of responsibilities, including: content producers that are responsible for producing civic orientation content (e.g. text, media); tutor that are responsible for teaching civic orientation; coordinators that are responsible for coordinating activities of teaching and content distribution. Tutors in particular, are a heterogeneous group of practitioners due to their background, culture, language, education, and worldviews in general (e.g. beliefs). Furthermore, the tutors do not share a common knowledge domain (e.g. formal education), pedagogies for teaching, and they are all responsible for teaching a particular group of newcomers through their native language.

Subsequently, the integration workers were involved in a process of continuous work-integrated learning, where they actively participated in iterative cycles of design and evaluation of proposed E-Learning solutions. The E-Learning solutions were thus implemented and tested through a work-integrated philosophy [11] [14], which enabled a linkage between theoretical underpinnings of E-Learning at work [10], the use of the integration workers' practical and experiential know-how (e.g. areas of responsibilities), and a continuous reflection and learning. This process of work-integrated learning generated significant learning outcomes, which helped us address the E-learning solutions as adaptable E-Learning, and subsequently, to address the integration workers as heterogeneous groups of work-integrated learners.

B. *Adaptable E-Learning Solutions*

Based on our learning outcomes, we identified and defined the following adaptable E-Learning solutions:

- **Adaptable levels of distribution**: E-Learning content that is distributed on various levels of availability and authenticity. Different tutors need to access and manage different form of content for their sessions. Subsequently, E-Learning features need to be adaptable toward the heterogeneity of tutors and newcomers, with respect to factors such as language, culture, IT-literacy, and worldviews
- **Adaptable support of multimodality**: E-Learning features that are adaptable and support multimodal and large variation of IT-literacy among tutors and newcomers. For the tutors, this include features for content distribution; various pedagogies (e.g. online, classroom); modes of interaction (e.g. dialogues, instructions); customization of content (e.g. embedded learning objects). Whereas for the newcomers, E-Learning features need to be adapted toward newcomers' heterogeneity with respect to factors such as, language; culture; general IT-skills; handicaps (e.g. trauma due to war)
- **Adaptable space of collaboration:** E-Learning features that incorporate integration workers' communities of practice through collaborative features. These features include adaptable functionality for producing, maintaining, updating, and distributing content; scheduling of sessions; assessment; information distribution, and communication. An adaptable space, supported by a framework of IT-tools (see [28] for more information), were therefore designed and established to incorporate various forms of collaboration (e.g. content production, instructions) between the integration workers
- **Adaptable co-delivery and interaction**: E-Learning features that are adaptable toward co-delivering content and interaction with heterogeneous groups of participants such as the newcomers. This include features that incorporate adaptable mode of delivery (e.g. face-to-face, online, blended); adaptable modalities, text, graphics, picture, video; and adaptable modes of interaction (e.g. dialogues, online-instruction, video tutorial)
- **Adaptable content**: E-Learning features that enable production and delivery of content that is adaptable to cope with heterogeneous elements such as, age, education, literacy, gender, culture, norms and values, and worldviews (e.g. beliefs, prejudices, conceptions). E-Learning content shall thus be adaptable toward different levels of advancement such as, basic modules (e.g. facts about society); advanced learning modules (e.g. exercises); personalized content that incorporates multimodality and different use of language

C. Heterogeneous Groups of Work-Integrated Learners

Based on the learning outcomes of introducing and implementing adaptable E-Learning for civic orientation, we used work-integrated learning knowledge (e.g. [11-15]) to theorize our learning outcomes. More specifically, we focused on theorizing an understanding about: (1) who the users of adaptable E-Learning are; (2) what makes them significant as users of adaptable E-Learning; and (3) how can this knowledge contribute to an overall discussion about heterogeneity in E-Learning.

Starting with the first point, we address users of adaptable E-Learning as heterogeneous groups of work-integrated learners. Here, we explicitly emphasize on the integration workers and their practice of civic orientation. They are heterogeneous due to their practice, roles, areas of responsibilities, education, and worldviews in general. They do for instance not share a common formal education, – as for instance teachers at universities do – noir do they have a generalized set of IT-skills. However, their development of skills, competencies, and knowledge, was incorporated through work-integrated learning. Such activities included, a progressive problem-solving orientation (e.g. updating online content); continuous evaluation of learning outcomes through real dialogues; learning tasks that lead integration workers to examine their work in light of the provided E-Learning features; integration of E-Learning features with face-to-face learning situations whenever possible.

The second point opens up for an epistemic discussion about the significance of heterogeneity among users of adaptable E-Learning. For instance, through work-integrated learning, we could encourage collaboration and knowledge exchange between the integration workers. From an epistemic perspective, this means that we helped a group of heterogeneous practitioners to share and exchange different knowledge perspectives, which incorporate their different domains of knowledge, areas of responsibilities, professional roles and expertise, etc. The dimension of heterogeneity is thus essential for making users of adaptable E-Learning, significant.

The third and final point problematizes the notion of users in E-Learning situations. A transition from a traditional notion of E-Learning users (e.g. students, teachers of higher education) to notion that comprises heterogeneous groups of users, motivates for E-Learning solutions that are in situ adaptable toward heterogeneity. Work-integrated learning as a process and philosophy, becomes thus a facilitator for integration of heterogeneous forms of representation and learning activities (e.g. training, discussing, using metaphors, audio, visual etc.), which support heterogeneous groups of practitioners. Henceforth, we propose to frame a notion of adaptable E-Learning users, as heterogeneous groups of work-integrated learners. As an implication, we argue that such framing enables E-Learning designers to re-think who the learners and users of their E-Learning solutions are, and how they can be supported through solutions of adaptable E-Learning.

IV. Conclusion

Understanding who the users of E-Learning at work are, is an important task in order to design sufficient E-Learning solutions. Traditional E-Learning solutions are experienced as stiff, narrowly framed, and too demanding for dynamic workplaces outside the context of higher education. Users of E-Learning at work are thus different than users of traditional E-Learning in higher education (e.g. students, teachers). Due to their differences, they tend to be heterogeneous with respect to their age, gender, education, culture, language, etc. This create demands and challenges on how well E-Learning solutions are designed toward heterogeneity of various kind.

In order to meet such demands and challenges, we suggest that E-Learning solutions need to be adaptable toward different kind of workplaces and practitioners. We therefore introduced the concept of adaptable E-Learning and proposed its essential features within a particular case. Subsequently, we used work-integrated learning as a philosophy and process to incorporate continuous learning activities, which help understanding and problematizing the dimension of heterogeneity. Our results were theorized into an understanding of adaptable E-Learning users, as heterogeneous groups of work-integrated learners. We impose to elaborate our notion of work-integrated learners by applying and evaluating this notion through further research.

References

[1] Bokhari. M.U, and Iqrar, A. "Open Source Tools: Empowered the E-Learning Pedagogy in Distance Education," 2011.

[2] Garrison, D. R. "E-Learning in the 21st Century: A Framework for Research and Practice," *Taylor and Francis*, 2011.

[3] CIHE (The Council for Industry and Higher Education). "Response to the Joint Consultation Document from HEFCE and the Learning and Skills Council," 2002.

[4] DfES (Department for Education and Skills). "Education and Skills: Delivering Results a Strategy to 2006," *TSO, Norwich*, 2001.

[5] European Commission. "ELearning Conference Conclusions. Brussels: European Commission," 2005.

[6] Harun, M. H. "Integrating E-Learning into the Workplace," *The Internet of Higher Education*, Vol. 4(3-4), pp. 301-310, 2001.

[7] Slotte, V., and Tynjälä, P. "Industry-University Collaboration for Continuing Professional Development," *Journal of Education and Work*, Vol. 16(4), pp. 445-464, 2003.

[8] Burgess, J. R. D. "The Effectiveness of Distance Learning Initiatives in Organizations," *Journal of Vocational Behavior*, Vol. 63, pp. 289-303, 2003.

[9] DeRouin, R. E., Fritzsche, B. A., and Salas, E. "Learner Control and Workplace E-Learning: Design, Person, and Organizational Issues," J. Martocchio (Ed.), *Research in Personnel and Human Resources Management*, Vol. 24, pp. 181-214, New York, 2005.

[10] Tynjälä, P., and Häkkinen, P. "E-Learning at Work: Theoretical Underpinnings and Pedagogical Challenges," *Journal of Workplace Learning*, Vol. 17(5-6), 2005.

[11] Billett, S. "Learning Through Work: Workplace Participatory Practices," *Workplace Learning in Context*, pp. 109-125, 2004.

[12] Argyris, S., and Schön, D. A. "Organizational Learning II: Theory, Method, and Practice," *Addison-Wesley*, 1996.

[13] Billett, S. "Workplace Pedagogic Practices: Co-Participation and Learning," *British Journal of Educational Studies*, Vol. 50, No. 4, pp. 457-483, 2002.

[14] Eraut, M., Alderton, J., Cole, G., and Senker, P. "Learning from Other People at Work," *Supporting Lifelong Learning*, Vol. 1, pp. 127-145, 2002.

[15] Tynjäle, P. "Perspectives into Learning at the Workplace," *Educational Research Review*, 2008.

[16] Chen, B., Wang, M., Moormann, J., Olaniran, B. A., and Chen, N. S. "The Effects of Organizational Learning Environment Factors on E-Learning Acceptance," *Computers & Education*, 58(3), pp. 885-899, 2012.

[17] Admiraal, W., and Lockhorst, D. "E-Learning in Small and Medium-Sized Enterprises Across Europe: Attitudes Towards Technology, Learning, and Training," *International Small Business Journal*, 27(6), pp. 743-767, 2009.

[18] Wang, M., Vogel, D., and Ran, W. "Creating a Performance-Oriented E-Learning Environment: A Design Science Approach," *Information & Management*, 2011.

[19] Salas, E., Kosarzycki, M. P, Burke, C. S., Fiore, S. M., and Stone, D. L. "Emerging Themes in Ditance Learning Research and Practice, Some Food for Thought," *International Journal of Management Reviews*, Vol. 4, pp. 135-153, 2002.

[20] Welsh, E. T., Wanberg, C. R., Brown, E. G., and Simmering, M. J. "E-Learning: Emerging Uses, Empirical Results and Future Directions," *International Journal of Training and Development*, Vol. 7, pp. 245-258, 2003.

[21] Freund, R. J. "Mass Customization and Multiple Intelligence," *Keynote Speech at the International Conference on Mass Customization and Personalization*, 2004.

[22] Lave, J., and Wenger, E. "Situated Learning: Legitimate Peripheral Participation," *Cambridge University Press*, 1991.

[23] Wenger, E. "Communities of Practice: Learning, Meaning, and Identity," *Cambridge University Press*, 1998.

[24] Schön, D. "The Reflective Practitioner," *Temple Smith*, 1983.

[25] Schön, D. A. "Educating the Reflective Practitioner," *Jossey-Bass*, 1987.

[26] Nonaka, I., and Takeuchi, H. "The Knowledge-Creating Company: How Japanese Companies Create the Dynamics of Innovation," *Oxford University Press*, 1995.

[27] Haj-Bolouri, A., and Svensson, L. "Designing for Heterogeneous Groups of End-Users: Towards a Nascent Design Theory," In *Proceedings of World Conference on E-Learning in Corporate, Government, Healthcare, and Higher Education*, pp. 746-754, 2014.

[28] Haj-Bolouri, A., Bernhardsson, L., and Bernhardsson, P. "CollaborGeneous: A Framework of Collaborative IT-Tools for Heterogeneous Groups of Learners," *New Horizons in Design Science*, 2015.

[29] Haj-Bolouri, A., Berhnardsson, L., Bernhardsson, P., and Svensson, L. "An Information Systems Design Theory for Adaptable E-Learning," In *49th Hawaii International Conference on System Sciences* (HICSS), 2016.

[30] Haj-Bolouri, A., Chandra-Kruse, L., Iivari, J., and Flensburg, P. "How Habermas' Philosophy Can Inspire the Design of Information Systems: The Case of Designing an Open Learning Platform for Social Integration," *Selected Papers of the IRIS*, Issue No. 7, 2016.

Authors

Haj-Bolouri, Amir is a doctoral student in Information Systems with a specialization of Work-Integrated Learning at University West, Trollhättan, Sweden (e-mail: amir.haj-bolouri@hv.se).

Svensson, Lars is a full professor in Information Systems at University West, Trollhättan, Sweden (e-mail: lars.svensson@hv.se).

Manuscript received 15 March 2018. (Write the date on which you submitted your paper for review.) This work was supported in part by the U.S. Department of Commerce under Grant BS123456 (sponsor and financial support acknowledgment goes here).

Published as submitted by the author(s).

3D Printing of Biomimetic Scaffold for Annulus Fibrosus Regeneration

Thomas Christiani[1], Andrea Vernengo[2]
[1]Biomedical Engineering, Rowan University, Glassboro, NJ, [2]Chemical Engineering, Rowan University, Glassboro, NJ

This work focuses on the development of an advanced scaffold for tissue engineering of the annulus fibrosus (AF) of the intervertebral disc (IVD). Commonly, AF scaffold materials are made from fibrous electrospun polymers or silk. However, 3D printing, which has not yet been applied to AF repair, is advantageous for attaining complex scaffold custom geometries and region-specific printing of cells, polymers, and biomolecules within the material. In this work, multi-layer scaffolds (Figure 1A) were 3D printed by depositing polycaprolactone (PCL) struts in opposing angular orientations of ±30°, replicating the angle-ply arrangement of the native AF tissue. Models were made as standard tessellation language (STL) files and printed on a Robo 3D R1 (Robo, San Diego, CA). Commercially available PCL filament (Mn=72,000, diameter 1.75 mm) was extruded at 120°C and deposited onto a stationary platform maintained at 37°C. Scaffolds were printed with a strut diameter and parallel spacing between the struts of 800 and 1200 µm, respectively. For the cell study, AF cells were extracted from bovine caudal IVDs and expanded. First-passaged cells were seeded over collagen-coated scaffolds (each approx. 5x3x4mm) at a density of 40,000 cells/scaffold and cultured in Dulbecco's modified Eagle's medium (DMEM) supplemented with 10% fetal bovine serum and 1% penicillin/streptomycin. At day 21, scaffolds were stained with Alexa Fluor 647 phalloidin to visualize cell body shape. Immunofluorescence analysis was used to detect expression of collagen type I, collagen type II, and the AF-specific marker tenomodulin (TNMD). Confocal microscopy results indicate that the cells were able to attach and spread randomly on the PCL scaffolds. The AF cells stained positive for TNMD (Figure 1B) and expressed Collagen I predominantly. Overall, results demonstrate the feasibility of using this novel scaffold for AF cell culture and potential for its use in IVD tissue engineering. Future work will examine modifying the surface topography to induce biomimetic alignment of the AF cells.

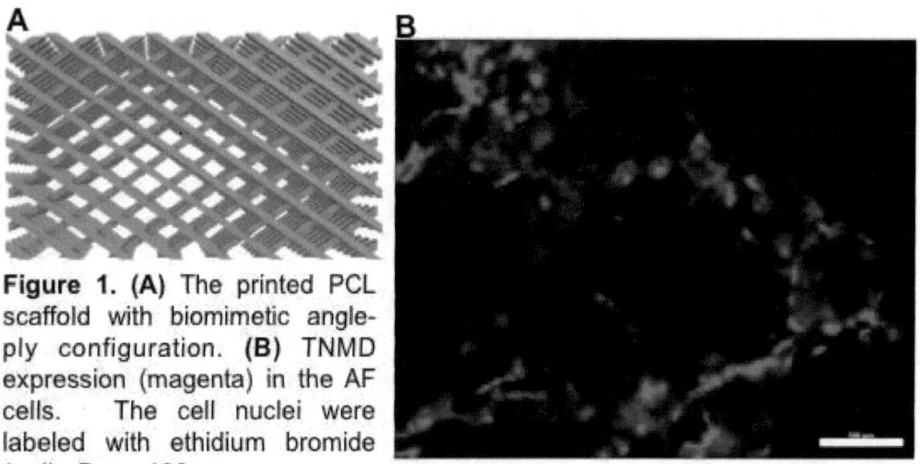

Figure 1. (A) The printed PCL scaffold with biomimetic angle-ply configuration. **(B)** TNMD expression (magenta) in the AF cells. The cell nuclei were labeled with ethidium bromide (red). Bar = 100 µm.

Co-construction of Knowledge in Work-Integrated E-learning Courses in Joint Industry-University Collaboration

Monika Hattinger and Kristina Eriksson[1]

[1]University West, Department of Engineering Science, Trollhattan, Sweden

Abstract— **Blended e-learning in higher education targeting company knowledge needs, can support continuous competence development for practitioners in the manufacturing industry. However, designing for such efforts are technically hard but even more challenging when the design aim to stimulate collaborative learning activities that bring in practitioners work experiences as a valuable knowledge source in construction with other peers or teachers. How are practitioners' experiences and research teachers' knowledge co-constructed and integrated in case-based methodologies? This article examines three types of case-based methodologies with purpose to stimulate mutual knowledge construction. The studies take part in a longitudinal joint industry-university project from 2014 until 2016. Twelve courses were analyzed through focus group sessions with 119 practitioners from 15 different companies. Results show that 1) Virtual digital cases stimulate high technology learning but low collaboration with peers, 2) On-line collaborative negotiations both stimulate web-conferencing and high interactivity, and 3) Real workplace cases do not stimulate e-learning (low use), but stimulate high work-integrated learning and knowledge expansion.**

Index Terms—**Co-construction, work-integrated e-learning, case-based methodology, manufacturing industry.**

I. Introduction

University e-learning education aims to support lifelong learning for practitioners in the manufacturing industry and strengthen their competence development integrated in work practice [1, 2]. However, traditional higher education courses are usually designed for individuals on campus and do not support work practitioners working full time. University campus courses are traditioinally not designed for time independence, flexibility or collaborative e-learning [3]. Furthermore, they do not include practitioners' knowledge based on their work experiences as a valuable source in knowledge construction with other peers and teachers. It is a demanding process to integrate practitioners' workplace experiences as a valuable knowledge source when designing e-learning courses. Particularly it is hard to make useful choices of learning technologies that support a case-based approach including practitioners' experienced-based knowledge.

The aim of this study is to explore how engineering practitioners and research teachers mutually co-construct knowledge in a case-based methodology. The research teachers are primarily performing production technology research and only part-time engage in teaching on advanced level. The practitioners are operators and expert engineers in the workplace. Given this, we explore the concept of co-construction of knowledge between practitioners' and research teachers' collaboration in e-learning courses through various forms of case-based methodologies. In the courses, different case-based methodologies are introduced to trigger different perspectives and learning in and through co-construction. The empirical context is a new type of course concept developed within the industry-university collaborative project ProdEx, and offers a new educational practice, see Figure 1. In the figure's lower left corner, post-secondary practical education is found. The lower right corner show post-secondary higher vocational education (a Swedish model). In the upper left corner we find distance and on-line higher education defined by the university that targets individual students. These types are established forms in Sweden.

The ProdEx project comprises a network of industries and one university collaborating in a longitudinal design and implementation process of blended and work-integrated e-learning courses, since 2013. The blended e-learning courses are designed towards manufacturing industry target knowledge content for an effective and competitive production in a digitalized industry 4.0 [4]. Research in the project has explored e-learning activities and co-construction of knowledge in various forms, and between different actors; industry managers, industry practitioners and university research teachers [5].

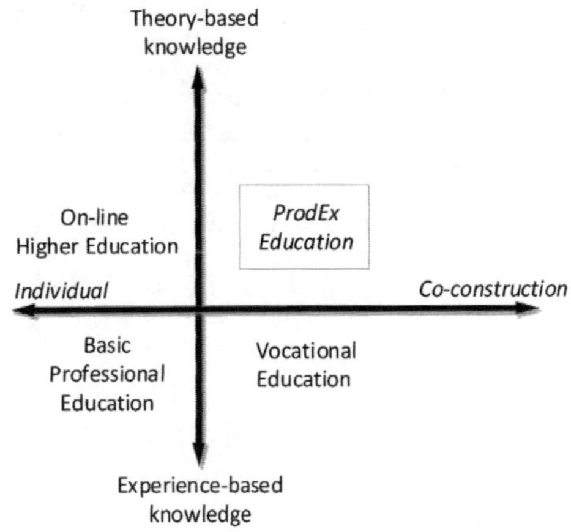

Figure 1. ProdEx positioned among other professional educational models.

II. RELATED RESEARCH

In a knowledge-based economy, manufacturing companies constantly need to strive for a flexible and cost-effective production, meanwhile delivering high quality products and costumer services in short-time [6]. Consequently, efforts with learning and educational projects across industry and university is a powerful way of integrating theory and practice in a process of co-construction of production technology knowledge. Tynjälä [7] put forward that scholastic learning should adopt specific features of workplace learning and workplace development of expertise.

A. *Co-construction of Knowledge*

There is today an ongoing debate on policy levels of the value of co-production, but little evidence on its value for professional work, expertise and knowledge [8, 9]. However, what happens in the concrete practices of such arrangements is less well known. Therefore we argue for a more practice-based approach through the concept of co-construction of knowledge [5]. Co-construction is open-ended between actors, and is the joint creation of a form, interpretation, activity, identity, skill, emotion, or other culturally meaningful realities [10]. The concept of co-construction contextualizes sharing, and giving from two or more perspectives. Further, the concept involves a social space in and between individuals, and across individuals and technological artifacts that prosper positive engagement and a certain excitement of new knowledge and learning [11-13]. This paper delineate how co-construction is developing between experienced industry practitioners and researchers in an e-learning practice.

B. *Engineering Competences and Work-Integrated Learning*

Engineering work is also about problem solving, improvement and continuous technological development. The production systems are highly automated and therefore engineering work consists of monitoring and controlling. However, reality is still far from an effective and fully digitalized work environment and new competences need to be strengthen continuously. Knowledge-intensive work pressure operators, engineers and manufacturing companies to assess new expert knowledge and adapt to changes that imply short-term flexibility instead of long-term perspectives [6].

To find sources and collaborations outside the company for strengthening practitioners integrated in work is one way for competence development [14]. Work-integrated learning (WIL) can be described as a combination of education and practice integrated in work. Work-integrated learning offers a combination of engineering education with engineering work practice on equal grounds for qualitative learning and knowledge development [7, 15-18].

III. RESEARCH CONTEXT AND METHOD

This paper is built on data collected within the ProdEx project, started in spring 2013 and will continue until spring 2020. About 25 different industry companies within the automotive and aerospace sector are engaged in a joint collaboration with a Swedish university. The industry network and the university collaborate around; competence mapping of engineering knowledge content, discuss implications for e-learning design of courses, and share the objective of strengthening expert engineering competences for future digitalized industrial work [19].

The different case-based methodologies explored are designed within 12 short university e-learning courses of 2.5 European Credits (ECTS), within the project ProdEx (Expert in Production Technology).

Figure 2. An industrial robot at PTC in Trollhättan.

A general ProdEx course of 2.5 ECTS is designed by:

Schedule: 5-6 weeks with maximum 2-4 lecture days at the Production Technology Centre (PTC, a laboratory center connected to the university). Additional web-conferences between the lectures are scheduled weekly.

Course material and tasks: instructional videos, authentic industry cases mixed with academic assignments, virtual and physical labs, written instructions, Power Points, books, articles. Materials published on the university LMS (learning management system) DisCo.

Communication and interactions through DisCo, chat and web-conferencing (Adobe Connect and Skype for business).

Examination through home assignments and case-methodologies, both digital and physical labs and cases. No written final exams.

Pedagogical philosophy: pedagogical strategies that activate participants constructing and contributing to the course. Bringing in their authentic and proven experiences closely related to personal skills and the companies' production processes. This is viewed as a work-integrated learning pedagogical philosophy.

Courses comprise the knowledge subjects; *industrial automation and machine security*, *negotiation skills for businesses*, and *machining and tribology*.

To incorporate and strengthening the practitioners as part of the mutual knowledge construction within the courses, three different case-based methodologies were analyzed that variously aimed to activate co-construction of knowledge between peers (see Examination above). The study focus is on practitioners becoming active learning participants and how they mutually engage their knowledge contribution [20]. The case methodology was developed during design cycles of 12 courses from 2014 until 2016, as part of the whole course design inspired by the Action Design Research (ADR) (Sein et al., 2011).

Three case methodologies are included; Virtual digital case, Online collaborative negotiations and Real workplace case.

A. Data collection

The data collection was conducted by twelve focus group sessions, performed on the last course day after the final examination. Each session creates a unique intervention and forms a meaning unit, in which participants' together can verbalize their meanings, knowledge views and negotiate through group interactions [21].

The sessions were performed in forms of open discussions to trigger practitioners' experiences of the course interventions. A semi-structured interview guide [22] was directing the open-ended dialogues followed by broad themes of e-learning technologies, communication, course format/modality, teacher support, examination, competence areas, work-integrated learning and future competence needs. The courses are categorized into three themes according to their specific knowledge subjects, see Table 1.

KNOWLEDGE SUBJECTS (THEMES)	COURSE SESSIONS	SESS-IONS	PARTICI-PANTS
Automation	Industrial Automation (4) Machine Security in Robotics (1)	5	44
Business	Negotiations Skills (3)	3	34
Mechanical Engineering	Machining (3) Tribology (1)	4	41
Summary		**12**	**119**

TABLE I. KNOWLEDGE SUBJECTS SORTED IN THREE COURSE THEMES

IV. ANALYSIS AND RESULTS

To answer the research question of how practitioners' experiences and research teachers' knowledge are co-constructed and integrated in case-based methodologies, the transcripts were read through, coded and categorized the excerpts into a scheme with the overall category case methodologies, i.e. performed through a content analysis [21]. Codes were created continuously with support of the Quality Data Analysis system NVivo 11. The data was organized into the three knowledge subjects, see Table I. Three main categories turned out to be helpful to organize the results, Problems, Active learning and Work-integrated learning, in which we delineated how co-construction was developing. Through the excerpts we found what and how work-experiences and learning experiences were triggered within the three case methodologies. Results from the analysis together with a description of the three cases setup follow below.

A. Virtual digital cases

The case is a digital lab, designed and implemented by the software Camtasia and run on a single PC. The case aim to strengthening learning of PLC programming at an individual level. It includes PLC logics and tasks around solutions of how to perform various solutions. After a week of solving the case, participants meet in a Skype-conference session, discussing various questions and how they made their own solutions.

A problem raised is illustrated:

Operator 3: *"I felt I would have enjoyed some more basic facts when you sit at home and do these assignments. How do these things really work? It was a fairly steep curve when you started with this."*

However, other more experienced practitioners meant the case was activating learning.

Active learning is shown as:

Operator 5: *"It* [the virtual lab] *was very good."*

Another operator raised the importance of advancing their skills:

Operator 1: *"We've historically worked with this kind of programming so I think it's perfect. This is useful teaching material, and it's also cheaper. With time you build more models. So that you can advance..."*

They reflect on their own lack of theoretical knowledge from before, but eventually how they advance through working with the case, in iterations. Both individually and through negotiating it on-line with peers and research teachers.

Work-integrated learning is shown here:

Interviewer: Did you learn anything?

Engineer 1: *"Yes, it (the virtual lab) was good, you got to work a lot yourself."*

Operator 4: *"To get a foundation and to understand how it actually works, for instance when the PLC sends out signals and codes."*

Operator 2: *"We will have extremely many signals in a machine controlled by PLC. At least in the lathe."*

They integrate and affirm their knowledge more in-depth, of how a PLC can be programmed and variations of how it can be useful for new work practices.

B. On-line collaborative negotitations

On-line collaborative negotiations were practiced through a predefined Harvard Case (H-case). The case was designed as an intervention with six participant roles, taking part during three hours. The chair had to keep track of time and direct the negotiations. The case can be solved in multiple ways and is usually hard to find a solution that reach a compromise between all six parties. This is an in-built pedagogy. We found that different groups had various strategies for solving the case. In some groups, discussions were loud, and in others, voices were only raised during certain phases to achieve as reasonable result as possible.

During the H-case, many participants felt they lacked time to negotiate with everybody and to consider different alternative solutions before voting according to their choices. Some felt that the initial written instructions were unclear on how to "perfectly" perform the case whereas others meant that the case lacked some authenticity.

Problems raised are illustrated:

Purchaser 2: "*We should have practiced much more IRL before the web-conferencing... not many of us followed the instructions.*"

Purchaser 1: *"No, it was more like a game...more like playing monopoly. We practiced a lot of lobbyism by writing in the web forum. Not the kind of lobbyism that happens in a real meeting."*

They are really negative towards the use of web-conferencing for handling negotiations and questioned the assigned roles in the H-case. Even if they had experiences of web-conferencing, they were not familiar with negotiation situations with customers and suppliers in web-conferencing media. It seems that the industry purchasers want particular instructions from the research teachers' along with pre-defined instructions, to be able to come to closure. The design of the H-case is that it will almost never solved, because there are over 100 various solutions and hence no precise answer at the end, such as in real life. To overcome these problems and to realize the potential for active learning, meaning their new negotiation skills, they started to reflect upon their own learning.

Active learning is shown as:

Operator 2: *"I think this really was an awesome H-case to learn so much in so short time, I am impressed."*

Another operator [3] follows up, and describes that:

"During a business negotiation, one needs to be calm, to not always claim to be right, rather to show appreciation of other perspectives than your own."

Participants reflect further upon the intertwining of theory and practice.

Operator 4: *"In real life, there is more background information... Now there was only the written instructions, so you had to invent things on your own."*

Following these discussions, triggered by the H-case, participants were engaged to integrate new knowledge integrated in work.

Work-integrated learning is shown here:

Operator 1: *"My manager asks a lot and is actively engaged. I really have learnt new stuff from this type of soft skills course because I am aiming to transform my position from CAM-operator into becoming a service technician."*

Human knowing and experience based knowledge was intertwined with new negotiation skills knowledge through the H-case. Through mutual discussions between the practitioners in the focus groups, they were able to solve problems independently, even if they experienced that some case instructions were unclear.

They also highlighted that they had started to reflect more on themselves, and their own actions and talking, towards other people. They felt they could apply what they learnt in their work, and were satisfied with their personal development as part of future transformative actions in their work practice.

C. Real workplace cases

A turning and milling case, was to be managed and solved at the home company. They were supposed to get written and oral instructions from the research teacher. However, the instructions and prerequisites were either late communicated or solely orally gone through by the teacher. To be able to do the real workplace lab case, the participants had to interrupt the daily manufacturing processes at the home factory.

Problems raised are illustrated as:

Consultant 1: *"We did not have time to find equipment to perform the lab. However, if the labs had been here at PTC I think it would have been easier."*

Operator 2: *"We did not know it was pre-requisite to have a turning and milling machine at the home company."*

Even if there were problems to perform the lab, the task showed results that were deviating far from traditional campus solutions and new innovative solutions occurred.

Active learning is shown as:

Operator 2: *"You must have your own machine, the material, and also tools to test. These are the prerequisites, otherwise you cannot solve the task."*

Operator 6: *"However, the benefit was to take an example from the own factory."*

The problem situation with the turning and milling lab and accessibility to machines, evolved into suggestions on how the course could get showcases of a "perfect way of doing digital labs."

Consultant 1: *"It was nice labs, but only if you were able to perform them..."*

Consultant 2: "*I think a good solution would be to web cast how to run the milling and turning machine. I mean to take a camera into the machine and make a video of how to perform it all and then put it on DisCo [LMS].*"

They want to have a certain defined solution to their lab, to make sure they perform it right. Some practitioners did therefore not perform the lab at all, because they had no experience of running such machines, which on the other hand was not mandatory before the course started.

Work-integrated learning is shown here:

Operator 6: *"Think we learned a good part from the demos that other participants solved. I for sure want to go into the next course, Tribology (step II). My manager wants me to continue."'*

V. DISCUSSION AND CONCLUSION

The analysis of the longitudinal data, resulted in a broad variation of case methods as working tools for co-construction of knowledge. The cases activated both learning and contributions from the practitioners' which stimulated advancement of their skills. Analysis of the results also generated evidence of user-experiences of mediated discussions through the three case methodologies. The different cases aimed at integrating active learning between practitioners for future transformations in work practices [15]. The results illustrate that the design of the case methodologies both includes theory-based instruction and experience-based practices, see Figure 2.

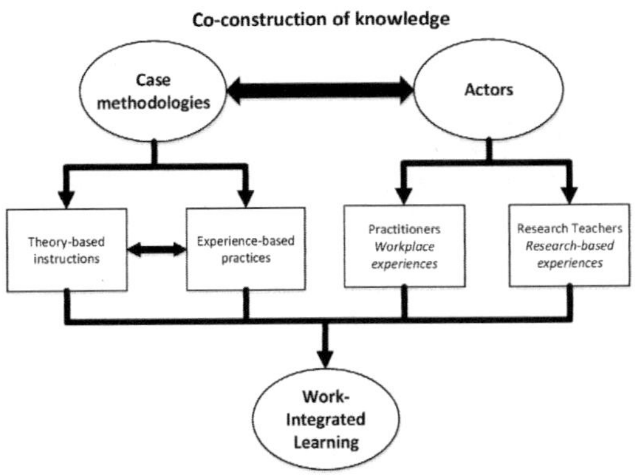

Figure 3. Overview of co-construction of knowledge through interactions between case methodologies and actors

The cases are triggered and evaluated by the actors (practitioners and research teachers) through their use during the course, and evaluation in the focus group sessions. Hence, both actors' experience (workplace vs research-based) were intertwined during the cases. Such intertwining stimulated co-construction and work-integrated learning.

The practitioners were co-constructing knowledge together actively in the courses and in the cases. Even if some case instructions were unclear, practitioners were, through negotiations of the course instructions and content, able to solve problems independently. The focus group sessions themselves also turned out to be a session for problem solving and for raising issues. The results among the practitioners show that they reached deeper learning, how to reflect on conflicting situations and the importance of taking time before decision making in future solutions within workplace situations. They also highlighted that they had started to reflect more on themselves, their own actions and talking, towards other people. They felt they could apply what they learnt in their work, and were satisfied with their personal development as part of future transformative actions in their work practice.

In focus groups there were discussions on the new course material, concerning old problems versus new solutions, which illustrated signs to stimulate actions into meaningful production [23]. The case-based approaches within the courses were loaded with signs to stimulate practitioners' intentionality and for them to feel comfortable to put forward, and contribute to new active learning built on their experience-based knowledge combined with new learning. The case-based approach in the courses therefore became a structured learning activity, that emphasized collaboration and knowledge sharing through co-construction including knowledge content and forms. This pedagogical strategy was stimulating co-construction of expert knowledge into mutual expertise. The courses became a joint collaborative adventure, and a respected activity for co-construction of expert knowledge. Overall results show that; Virtual digital cases stimulate high technology learning but low collaboration with peers, On-line collaborative negotiations stimulate web-conferencing and high interactivity, and Real workplace cases do not stimulate e-learning (low use), but stimulate high work-integrated learning and knowledge expansion.

This paper contributes to an understanding of a process of mutual and co-constructive learning between the practitioners and the research teachers, leading to new knowledge insights for the practitioners' work practice. Hopefully this will influence future work-integrated transformations. We therefore argue that co-construction of knowledge, between practitioners and research teachers, can be encouraged within blended e-learning courses through collaborative case-based methodologies.

REFERENCES

[1] Fischer, G., "*Lifelong learning-more than training.*" *Journal of Interactive Learning Research*, 2000. 11(3): p. 265.

[2] Laurillard, D., "*Rethinking university teaching: A conversational framework for the effective use of learning technologies.* " 2013: Routledge.

[3] Dubois, C. and L. Long, "Improving the Design of Workplace E-Learning Research." *International Journal on E-Learning*, 2012. 11(4): p. 419-440.

[4] Madsen, E.S., A. Bilberg, and D.G. Hansen. "*Industry 4.0 and digitalization call for vocational skills, applied industrial engineering, and less for pure academics.*" in 5th World Conference on Production and Operations Management P&OM. 2016.

[5] Hattinger, M., "*Co-constructing Expertise: Competence Development through Work-Integrated e-Learning in joint Industry-University Collaboration.* " PhD Thesis, 2018, University West.

[6] Schmiede, R. and M.C. Will-Zocholl, "Engineers' work on the move: challenges in automobile engineering in a globalized word." *Engineering Studies*, 2011. 3(2): p. 101-121.

[7] Tynjälä, P., "Perspectives into learning at the workplace." *Educational research review*, 2008. 3(2): p. 130-154.

[8] Fenwick, T., *Co-production in professional practice: a sociomaterial analysis.* Professions and professionalism, 2012. 2(2): p. 1-16.

[9] Needham, C., "Realising the potential of co-production: negotiating improvements in public services." *Social Policy and Society*, 2008. 7(2): p. 221-231.

[10] Jacoby, S. and E. Ochs, "*Co-construction: An introduction.*" 1995, Taylor & Francis.

[11] Rice, M.P., "Co-production of business assistance in business incubators: an exploratory study." *Journal of business venturing*, 2002. 17(2): p. 163-187.

[12] Weinberger, A. and F. Fischer, *A framework to analyze argumentative knowledge construction in computer-supported collaborative learning.* Computers & education, 2006. 46(1): p. 71-95.

[13] Goldstein, L.S., *The relational zone: The role of caring relationships in the co-construction of mind.* American Educational Research Journal, 1999. 36(3): p. 647-673.

[14] Hattinger, M., et al., *E-learning Readiness and Absorptive Capacity in the Manufacturing Industry.* International Journal of Advanced Corporate Learning (iJAC), 2014. 7(3): p. pp. 33-40.

[15] Billett, S., "Knowing in practice: Re-conceptualising vocational expertise." *Learning and instruction*, 2001a. 11(6): p. 431-452.

[16] Eames, C. and C. Cates, "*Theories of learning in cooperative education.*" International handbook for cooperative education: An international perspective of the theory, research and practice of work-integrated learning, 2011(2nd ed.): p. 41-52.

[17] 17. Engeström, Y. and H. Kerosuo, *From workplace learning to inter-organizational learning and back: the contribution of activity theory.* Journal of Workplace Learning, 2007. **19**(6): p. 336-342.

[18] 18. Trede, F., *Role of work-integrated learning in developing professionalism and professional identity.* Asia-Pacific Journal of Cooperative Education, 2012. 13(3): p. 159-167.

[19] Hattinger, M. and K. Eriksson. "*Action Design Research: Design of e-WIL for the Manufacturing Industry*." in In proceedings of the Americas Conference on Information Systems, AMCIS 2015, Puerto Rico August 13-15, 2015. 2015.

[20] Pare, A. and C. Le Maistre, "Active learning in the workplace: transforming individuals and institutions." *Journal of education and work*, 2006. 19(4): p. 363-381.

[21] Graneheim, U.H. and B. Lundman, "Qualitative content analysis in nursing research: concepts, procedures and measures to achieve trustworthiness." *Nurse education today*, 2004. 24(2): p. 105-112.

[22] Bryman, A., "*Social research methods*." 4th ed. 2012, New York: Oxford university press.

[23] Sannino, A., Y. Engeström, and M. Lemos, "Formative interventions for expansive learning and transformative agency." *Journal of the Learning Sciences*, 2016. 25(4): p. 599-633.

AUTHORS

Monika Hattinger, PhD in Informatics and Work-integrated learning and is with the department of Engineering science at University West, Trollhattan, Sweden (e-mail: monika.hattinger@ hv.se).

Kristina Eriksson, PhD in Mechnical Engineering and is with the department of Engineering science at University West, Trollhattan, Sweden (e-mail: kristina.eriksson@ hv.se)

Manuscript received March 14, 2018. This research was funded by the Swedish Knowledge Foundation (www.kks.se) and the Work-integrated learning research group at University West.

Published as submitted by the author(s)

3D-Printing Heterogeneous Porous Patterns in Tissue Engineered Bone Scaffolds

Aine O'Sullivan[1], Ethan Nyberg[1], Warren Grayson, PhD[1,2]
[1]Biomedical Engineering, Johns Hopkins University, Baltimore, MD, [2]Translational Tissue Engineering Center, Johns Hopkins University, Baltimore, MD

3D-printing biomaterial scaffolds offers a promising direction for treatment of large craniofacial defects, as it provides a customized patient-specific approach. An important aspect of 3D printed scaffolds is the porous space contained within them, which promotes optimal cell growth and regeneration of tissues within the scaffold. These properties are obtained by "slicing" a 3D volume into the desired patterns of pore geometries. Use of 3D-printing as a treatment option is limited by the inability of current slicing programs to use the full range of 3D-printer design space to produce highly defined porous geometries. Addition of gradient pore size and pore density would allow for manufacturing of more complex 3D-shapes. Tuning pore and strut size are of particular importance in achieving optimal tissue growth and mechanical strength.

We have designed a feature-driven MATLAB script that uses specified porous volumes to generate toolpath instructions for 3D-printing complex geometries. Using a Lulzbot 3D printer, we have been able to manufacture scaffolds from ABS over a range of pore sizes (0.2-1.2mm) and pore densities (5%-71%). We assessed scaffolds for print quality and mechanical properties, and found we were able to achieve a high degree of print fidelity for multiple pore diameters and densities. Mechanical testing showed that the scaffolds exhibited compressive moduli within the desired range, with modulus decreasing as porosity increased, as expected.

We then evaluated the boundary between different porous regions of the scaffolds and analyzed gradient and edge features produced by these different pore and strut sizes. Of particular importance is achieving a high degree of pore interconnectivity across these boundaries without sacrificing mechanical continuity of the scaffold. We have been able to vary the pore diameter up to steps of 0.6mm and the pore density in steps of up to 40% while still maintaining the desired boundary features. Using these designs, we have been able to also create gradients of pore geometries. These are heterogeneous patterns of pore properties that enable the creation of scaffolds that meet specific design requirements. Gradients are now being applied to the design and manufacturing of anatomic scaffolds such as a human-scale zygomatic arch scaffold.

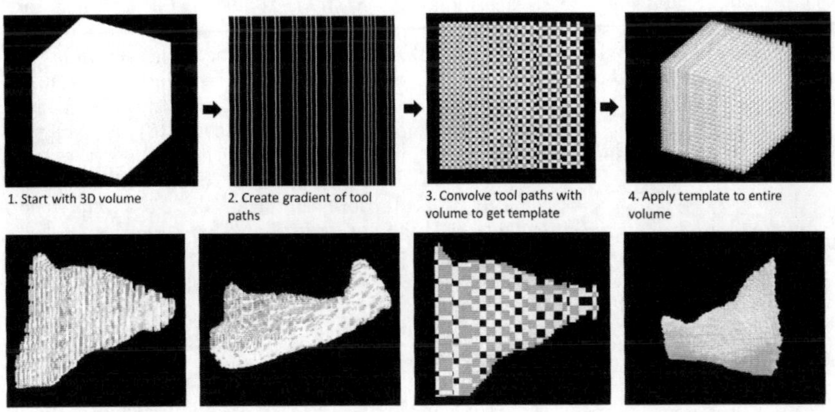

Figure 1: Work flow of applying gradient pore patterns to a 3D volume (top row). Examples of gradients applied to a zygomatic arch scaffold (bottom row).

Obstacles to using E-Learning in an Advanced Way

Annika Jokiaho[1], Birgit May[2], Marcus Specht[3] and Slavi Stoyanov[3]
[1] Ludwigsburg University of Education/E-Learning, Ludwigsburg, Germany
[2] University of Stuttgart/E-Learning, Stuttgart, Germany
[3] Open University Netherlands/Welten Institute, Heerlen, Netherlands

***Abstract*— E-Learning has become a common way to teach and learn. The number of technologies for a variety of educational purposes is already quite high and constantly rising. Scientific experiments and studies increasingly confirm the usefulness of various technologies for teaching purposes. Nevertheless, there is still a lack of formal training and support of digital skills within faculty training. Studies that report the potential of E-Learning are matched by those reporting the obstacles. Universities throughout Europe have now established Learning Management Systems (LMS); instead of using these to their full potential, lecturers often just upload their syllabus and some reading material. At the same time, higher education institutions all over Europe are expected to implement innovative technologies and scenarios such as Open Educational Resources (OER) or Massive Open Online Courses (MOOCs), but only a small number of universities actually do so. What are the reasons for not utilizing the pedagogic potentials of E-Learning? What findings does the current research provide on this topic? Which obstacles can be derived from studies and what can be done to avoid them? What are the individual obstacles of one institution or university? This contribution summarizes obstacles that were identified in recent studies and discusses possible solutions to finding connections between obstacles to mitigate the negative effects. It also describes a data collection method (group concept mapping) suitable for identifying the individual obstacles at an institution or university using a study in the European ERASMUS+ project AduLeT (Advanced Use of Technologies in Higher Education) as an example.**

***Index Terms*— E-Learning, Group Concept Mapping, Higher Education, Obstacles.**

I. Introduction

Most universities in Europe have been using Learning Management Systems (LMS) to enrich their face-to-face teaching [1], [2] and have specific departments for E-Learning [2], [3]. Nevertheless, for most higher education lecturers in Europe, E-Learning means uploading documents on the LMS [4], or generating content [5]. Only few lecturers use the pedagogic potentials of E-Learning [6]. While cooperative and collaborative scenarios are rarely used, higher education institutions, in particular, should be at the forefront of innovative teaching and learning scenarios with digital media. There are several obstacles preventing the establishment of new ways of teaching in higher education [7], leading to a discrepancy between expectations and reality. Several studies investigate the use of E-Learning [8], [9] or sustainability [10]. Only little research can be found concerning obstacles to using E-Learning. Mahmodi and Ebrahimzade [11] have investigated obstacles for students using E-Learning. Knowing the obstacles to using E-Learning can help to understand the situation at the individual university or workplace better. Therefore, this article summarizes obstacles identified in recent studies, and subsequently discusses possible approaches to overcoming these obstacles. Due to the diversity of universities and institutions, this article also describes a method of collecting the obstacles at different institutions with the group concept mapping (GCM) method. This article presents results from a literature review and a GCM study carried out within the framework of the European ERASMUS+ project AduLeT (Advanced Use of Technologies in Higher Education).

II. Methods

In order to identify obstacles to using E-Learning from the perspective of a lecturer, a literature review was conducted. The keywords used for the research within common educational databases were “barriers, obstacles, pitfalls” as well as “E-Learning, online-teaching, and learning management system”. Moreover, the studies had to fulfill the following criteria: the studies had to be conducted in the field of higher education, the studies had to have a focus on obstacles to using E-Learning for lecturers, as well as being empirical studies, and published in the year 2010 or later. Most of the studies are from the United States, such as the studies by Allen and Seaman [12], Bacow, Bowen, Guthrie, Lack, and Long [13], Baran [14], Dahlstrom, Brooks, and Bichsel [6], as well as Lloyd, Byrne, and McCoy [15]. There are only a few studies from Europe, such as Cabral, Pedro, and Gonçalves [16] from Portugal or Moscinska and Rutkowski [17] from Poland, and Sanchez, Hueros, and Ordaz [18] from Spain. These studies focus on finding obstacles to the use of E-Learning at one specific university. A review of literature from the United Kingdom can be found in Islam [19]. Three studies are from Africa, like the studies by Mutisya and Makokha [20] and Tarus, Gichoya, and Muumbo [21] from Kenya, as well as the study of Mwakyusa and Mwalyagile [22] from Tanzania. Studies investigating obstacles to using E-Learning in the Middle East can be found for Iraq in Al-Azawei, Parslow, and Lundqvist [23] for Iran in Farzaneh, Mousavi, and Maghabl [24], as well as Al-Shboul [25] from Jordan. Results from Australia can be found in the study of Anderson [26] and from Asia in Arinto for the Philippines [27].

The collection of obstacles from the literature review can be compared with the results of the GCM study.

The AduLeT project used the group concept mapping (GCM) method in the study. GCM [28] (see also [29], [30]), is a participative research methodology that facilitates a group of people arriving at a shared vision about a particular issue (e.g. problems with the use of ICT in teaching). The participants are asked to participate in a few commonly used activities such as generating ideas, sorting ideas into groups and rating ideas on some values (e.g. importance of problems with the use of ICT in teaching and difficulties in solving these problems). While the participants generate, sort and rate ideas individually, two advanced multivariate statistical techniques - multidimensional scaling (MDS) and hierarchical cluster analysis (HCA) - aggregate the individual contributions to identify patterns in the data. Visualizations of the results such as concept maps and pattern matches help to interpret the findings. GCM shows how ideas are related, how they are grouped in more general categories, and how much emphasis is given to each idea and cluster.

The procedure included the following steps:

(1) Idea generation. The participants were asked to brainstorm as many ideas as possible, completing the following focus prompt: "A problem for the use of ICT in my teaching is ..."

(2) Sorting the ideas. The participants were asked to group the ideas on similarity of meaning giving each group a name.

(3) Rating the ideas. The participants were asked to rate the ideas on (a) the relative importance of each statement about problems with using ICT in teaching, using a scale ranging from 1 (relatively unimportant) to 5 (very important); and (b) rate each statement on how difficult /easy it is to solve the problem with using ICT in teaching, applying a 1-to-5 scale where 1 = very difficult and 5 = very easy.

(4) Analysis of the data applying MDS, HCA, correlation and significant tests.

Within this article the results of step one and step two will be described. The analysis of step three and step four is still ongoing and will be part of future publications.

III. Results

A. *Obstacles identified in the literature*

The identified obstacles were divided into three different areas: personal factors, institutional and cultural factors, and technical factors. Personal factors include all obstacles that are dependent on the person. Institutional and cultural factors contain obstacles that are shaped by the institution and which lecturers cannot control. Technical obstacles refer to the use of technologies and infrastructure [4].

Personal factors: Time was mentioned in several studies (e.g. [14], [15], [19], [20], [26]). Specifically, the additional time needed for the preparation of E-Learning, is a major obstacle for lecturers, since there is generally more time needed than in face-to-face teaching [14], [15], [20]. Anderson [26] found in his study at a large Australian university that the flexible use of time in an online environment is also an advantage for lecturers experienced in E-Learning. For lecturers with less E-Learning experience, the lack of time is often a problem. The academic status might also have an impact. In a study with 386 lecturers from 36 colleges at a large state university system in the United States, Shea [31] found out that assistant, associate and full professors were more demotivated by the additional time needed for online teaching than part-time or non-traditional faculty such as instructors or teaching assistants. Lecturers with less experience with E-Learning seem to be less self-confident and have more doubts about their skills to teach online. Some respondents of the study by Anderson [26] were of the opinion that E-Learning is more time consuming, even if they had not yet tried it out themselves. Other respondents report a need for additional support. Lloyd, Byrne and McCoy [15] found that lecturers with less E-Learning experience generally rate obstacles higher in comparison to experienced users. Individual motivation is another personal factor in the use of E-Learning. The lack of motivation was mentioned as an obstacle in several of the studies (e.g. [14], [26]). Furthermore, support has an impact on the motivation of lecturers [14]. Anderson [26] found out that self-efficacy has a high impact on motivation. Self-efficacy again depends on previous experiences. Moreover, older studies show that age and employment status might have an impact on motivation. In the study by Shea [31], younger faculty (<45 years), in particular, had more doubts concerning the use of E-Learning due to lack of recognition of online teaching in their institution. By contrast, the flexibility of time by using E-Learning has the largest impact on the motivation of lecturers.

Institutional and cultural factors: From a lecturer's point of view, two obstacles concerning institutional and cultural factors were identified: support and recognition. At most higher education institutions, a variety of approaches are available for lecturers to support the use of E-Learning. Training courses are an essential part of the support. A wide range of topics should be offered in training courses, from using specific tools to pedagogical issues, in order to enable lecturers make advanced use of E-Learning [4], [23], [26]. The number of training courses attended seems to be a key factor in the degree of utilization of learning management systems [16]. Empty courses are much more likely to be found by lecturers that have not attended any training course. Lecturers that have taken part in three or even more training courses use the learning management system at a much higher level, technically as well as pedagogically. The lack of recognition of online teaching is an obstacle to using E-Learning (e.g. [13], [26]). Hence, Bacow et al., [13] suggest providing incentives for faculty, such as a stipend or reducing responsibilities in other areas. Since faculty time is the scarcest resource for lecturers, a financial incentive could be less appealing than having more time for developing E-Learning courses. In the study by Shea [31] the lack of recognition was even the biggest obstacle to using E-Learning at all.

Technical factors: Technical factors include skills in using E-Learning tools, usability, and infrastructure. There is wide agreement in the various studies that lecturers' existing competences influence the use of E-Learning (e.g. [6], [23]). The range of computer literacy required for the use of E-Learning tools in teaching is very wide. The basic level would be tasks such as uploading or storing files. However, the ways to use learning management systems are endless and an exhaustive use of all available options would not be expected [26]. Competent use however, requires knowledge of the learning management system, computer literacy [6], basic legal knowledge and pedagogical skills [4]. Therefore, it comes as no surprise that many teachers believe their teaching would be more effective if they had more skills in using the learning management system [6]. Inexperienced users are more likely to be afraid of the technology itself, of failure, or being embarrassed in front of the students [26]. A common technical obstacle is the lack of user-friendliness of learning management systems (e.g. [17], [26], [31]). Nowadays, many users are accustomed to the comfortable operation of social networks, such as writing comments or liking something. The handling of learning management systems is therefore often perceived as cumbersome [32]. The existing technical infrastructure has a significant impact on the use of E-Learning. This includes not only the reliability of the tools used and the IT support offered [13], [26], but also a stable Internet connection [23].

The literature review showed that technical factors represent an obstacle that should not be underestimated [6], [26]. Especially in the case of developing countries, the equipment at the universities is mentioned as an obstacle that hinders or prevents the use of E-Learning. In addition to the lack of equipment (e.g. computers, tablets, laptops), a lack of infrastructure (e.g. no stable WiFi connection) is an additional factor (e.g. [20], [21], [24]). This is important because technical factors also play an important role in the sustainability of E-Learning projects. McGill, Klobas, and Renzi [35] have analyzed 64 empirical studies about E-Learning projects and found out that the technologies in use must be updated early enough and always be up to date. In addition, the technologies must be reliable in order to facilitate sustainable use. A reliable infrastructure and skills in using the tools are necessary factors, while user-friendliness is a sufficient factor for the use of E-Learning. According to Lloyd, Byrne, and McCoy [15], lecturers' existing experience could be the key to removing obstacles. This aspect was previously neglected in the literature and would need to be examined more closely.

B. *Obstacles identified in the Group Concept Mapping Study*

A customized web-based environment was created specifically for the AduLeT project to facilitate data collection and analysis (Concept System Global Max) [33].

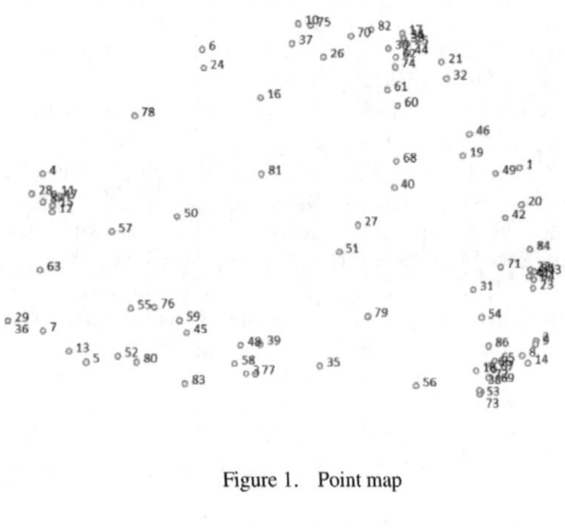

Figure 1. Point map

The first outcome of the GCM, is a point map which is a result of the MDS analysis (see Figure 1). It shows all the 87 reported obstacles and how they are related by locating similar terms close to each other in the two-dimensional space (a point map). MDS scaling also assigns each idea a bridging value (between 0 and 1) after computation of the map. A lower bridging value means more participants have grouped the statements with ideas around it. A higher bridging value indicates that the idea has been sorted together with statements further apart. MDS scaling also produces a statistic, called stress index (a value between 0 and 1) to indicate the goodness-of-fit between the mathematical model as represented by the point map and the raw sorting of the participants aggregated by a binary similarity matrix. In this project the stress value is 0.26, which is not only in the accepted range but it is also considered quite good in terms of the study's internal validity [34]. The next steps in the interpretation of the data was identifying thematic areas on the map by applying hierarchical cluster analysis (HCA).

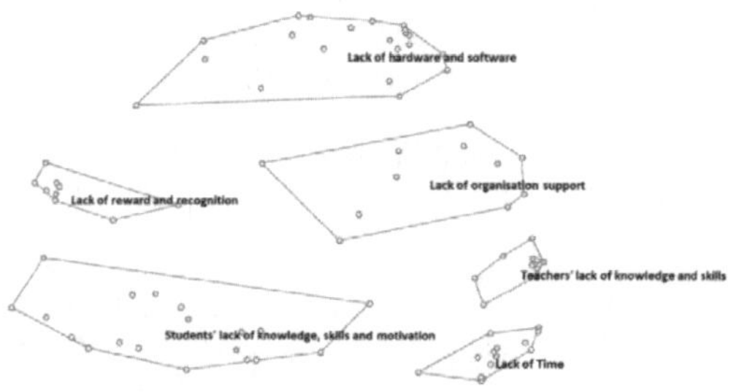

Figure 2. Obstacles categorized

The following issues regarding the use of E-Learning were identified: lack of organization support; teachers' lack of knowledge and skills; students' lack of knowledge, skills and motivation; lack of time; lack of hardware and software; and lack of reward and recognition (see Figure 2).

IV. Discussion and Conclusions

Although the literature review and GCM identified different categories of obstacles to adopting E-Learning, their findings are similar. Both methods have revealed issues related to availability of E-Learning tools, the need for technical and pedagogical support by organizations, insufficient time to learn E-Learning tools and implement them into teaching practice, teachers' low self-efficacy in educational technology knowledge and skills, and lack of recognition for the efforts teachers have made. A specific issue that the GCM has highlighted is shortage of knowledge, skills and motivation among students. Some more specific issues in this category are the need to adapt to learners' different levels of knowledge and skills, efforts to combine technology with effective teaching methods, and lack of appreciation from students. Teachers' low level of motivation as identified in the literature review, did not appear as a separate cluster in the GCM study but all other barriers depicted in the study negatively affect the motivation of teachers to apply E-Learning applications.

In the future we are going to analyse how the participants rate the obstacles on importance and easy/difficult to be overcome. In addition, we compare ratings of different groups of participants and identify long- and short-term measures.

ACKNOWLEDGMENT

The AduLeT project is funded by the ERASMUS+ Programme of the European Union.

REFERENCES

[1] Arbeitskreis E-Learning der ZKI (Zentren für Kommunikation und Informationsverarbeitung in Lehre und Forschung e.V.), *"ZKI LMS-Umfrage"*, April 21 2018, http://www.doodle.com/uyvcg2wz6s4bwv6v.

[2] M. Gaebel, V. Kupriyanova, R. Morais, and E. Colucci, *"E-Learning in European Higher Education Institutions"*, Brussels: European University Association, 2014.

[3] K. Seitz, K., *E-Learning Einrichtungen an deutschsprachigen Hochschulen*, Weblog post, August 2 2011, http://blog. E-Learning.tu-darmstadt.de/2011/08/02/e-learning-einrichtungen-an-deutschsprachigen-hochschulen/.

[4] A. Jokiaho, A. & B. May, "Hindernisse für die Nutzung von E-Learning an Hochschulen: Aktueller Forschungsstand", in C. Igel. Ed., *Bildungsräume*, pp. .20–31, Münster: Waxmann, 2017.

[5] M. Brown, J. Dehoney, & N. Millichap, *The next generation digital learning environment*, April 27 2015, https://library.educause.edu/resources/2015/4/the-next-generation-digital-learning-environment-a-report-on-research.

[6] E. Dahlstrom, D.C. Brooks, & J. Bichsel, *The current ecosystem of learning management systems in higher education: student, faculty, and IT perspectives*. Research report. Louisville, CO: ECAR, 2014, https://net.educause.edu/ir/library/pdf/ers1414.pdf.

[7] European Commission, Report to the European Commission on new modes of learning and teaching in higher education, European Union: Luxembourg, 2014.

[8] W. Bowen, M. Chingos, K. Lack, & T. Nygren, "Online learning in higher education", *EducationNext*, vol. 13, pp. 59–64, 2013.

[9] P. Taylor, K. Parker, A. Lenhart, & E. Patten, E., *The Digital Revolution and Higher Education*, 2011, http://www.pewinternet.org/files/old-media/Files/Reports/2011/PIP-Online-Learning.pdf.

[10] T.J. McGill, J.E. Klobas, & S. Renzi, "Critical success factors for the continuation of e-learning initiatives", *Internet and Higher Education*, vol. 22, 24–36, 2014.

[11] M. Mahmodi, & I. Ebrahimzade, "The Analysis of Iranian Students' Persistence in Online Education", *International Review of Research in Open and Distributed Learning*, vol. 16, pp. 98–119, 2015.

[12] I.E. Allen, J. & Seamann, Grade Level: Tracking Online Education in the United States, 2015, http://www.onlinelearningsurvey.com/reports/gradelevel.pdf.

[13] L.S. Bacow, G.B.Bowen, K.M. Guthrie, K.A. Lack, & M.P. Long, *Barriers to Adoption of Online Learning Systems in U.S. Higher Education*. New York: Ithaka, 2012.

[14] E. Baran, The transformation of online teaching practice: Tracing successful online teaching in higher education, Dissertation Iowa State University, 2011.

[15] S. Lloyd, M. Byrne, & T. McCoy, "Faculty-perceived barriers of online education", *MERLOT Journal of Online Learning and Teaching*, vol. 8, March 2012 http://jolt.merlot.org/vol8no1/lloyd_0312.pdf.

[16] P.B. Cabral, N. Pedro, & A.M. Gonçalves, "LMS in higher education: analysis of the effect of a critical factor 'Faculty Training', World Academy of Science, Engineering and Technology, vol. 6, pp. 571–576, 2012.

[17] K. Moscinska, & j. Rutkowski, "Barriers to introduction of e-learning: a case study, in *Proceedings of 2011 IEEE Global Engineering Education Conference* (EDUCON) 04-06 April 2011—Princess Sumaya University for Technology in Amman, Jordan, pp. 460-465, 2011.

[18] R.A. Sanchez, A.D. Hueros, & M.G. Ordaz, "E-Learning and the University of Huelva: A Study of WebCT and the technological acceptance model". *Campus-Wide Information Systems*, vol. 30 pp. 135–160, 2013.

[19] N. Islam, M. Beer, & F. Slack, "E-Learning challenges faced by academics in higher education: A literature review", *Journal of Education and Training Studies*, vol. 3, pp. 102-112, 2015.

[20] D.N. Mutisya, G.L. & Makokha, "Challenges affecting adoption of e-Learning in public universities in Kenya", *E-Learning and Digital Media*, vol. 13 pp. 140-157, 2016.

[21] J.K. Tarus, D. Gichoya, D. & A. Muumbo, "Challenges of implementing e-Learning in Kenya: A case of Kenyan public universities", *International Review of Research in Open and Distributed Learning*, vol. 16, pp. 120-141, 2015.

[22] W.P. Mwakyusa, & N.V. Mwalyagile,"Impediments of e-Learning adoption in higher learning institutions of Tanzania: An empirical review, *Journal of Education and Practice*, vol.7, pp.152-160, 2016.

[23] A. Al-Azawei, A., P. Parslow, & K. Lundqvist, "Barriers and opportunities of e-Learning implementation in Iraq: Acase of public universities, *International Review of Research in Open and Distributed Learning*, vol. 17, pp. 126-146, 2016.

[24] M. Mohamadzadeh, J. Farzaneh, M. Mousavi, & R. Maghabl, "Challenges and strategies for e-Learning development in the University of Payam Noor in Iran". *Turkish Online Journal of Distance Education*, vol. 13, pp. 297–308, 2012.

[25] M. Al-Shboul, M., "The level of e-Learning integration at the University of Jordan: Challenges and opportunities. *International Education Studies*, vol. 6, pp. 93–113, 2013.

[26] C. Anderson, C., Barriers and enabler to teachers' adoption of online teaching at an Australian University, Dissertation RMIT University, 2012.

[27] P.B. Arinto, "Issues and challenges in open and distance e-Learning: Perspectives from the Philippines", *International Review of Research in Open and Distributed Learning.*, vol. 17, pp.162–180, 2016.

[28] M. Kane, M., & W.M.K. Trochim, *Concept mapping for planning and evaluation*, Thousand Oaks, CA: Sage, 2007.

[29] M. Scheffel, H. Drachsler, S., Stoyanov, & M. Specht, "Quality indicators for learning analytics", *Educational Technology and society*, vol. 17, pp. 117–132, 2014.

[30] S. Stoyanov, K. Jablokow, S. Rosas, I. Wopereis, & P. Kirschner, "Concept mapping: an effective method for identifying diversity and congruity in cognitive style", *Evaluation and Program Planning. Concept Mapping at 25 (special issue),* vol. 60, pp. 238–244, 2017, http://dx.doi.org/10.1016/j.evalprogplan.2016.08.015.

[31] P. Shea, "Bridges and barriers to teaching online college courses: A study of experienced online faculty in thirty-six colleges", *Online Learning Consortium*, vol. 11, pp. 73–128, 2007.

[32] E. White, *The LMS: Are we experiencing a sea-change*, April 16 2016, http://saffroninteractive.com/saffron-interactive-launches-the-lms-are-we-experiencing-a-sea-change-white-paper/.

[33] The Concept System® Global MAX™ (Build 2016.046.12) [Web-based Platform], Ithaca, NY. Available from http://www.conceptsystemsglobal.com, 2016.

[34] S.R. Rosas, & M. Kane, "Quality and rigor of the concept mapping methodology: a pooled study analysis". *Evaluation and Program Planning*, 35, 236-245, 2012.

[35] T.J. McGill, J.E. Klobas, & S. Renzi, "Critical success factors for the continuation of e-learning initiatives", *Internet and Higher Education*, vol. 22, pp. 24–36, 2014.

AUTHORS

A. Jokiaho is head of the E-Learning department and the coordinator of the AduLeT project, Ludwigsburg University of Education, Ludwigsburg GERMANY (e-mail: jokiaho@ph-ludwigsburg.de).

B. May was head of the E-Learning department and the coordinator of the AduLeT project, Ludwigsburg University of Education. She is now with the Department of E-Learning, University of Stuttgart, Stuttgart GERMANY (e-mail: birgit.may@tik.uni-stuttgart.de).

M. Specht is Professor of Advanced Learning Technologies and he currently heads the CELSTEC Learning Technology Labs at the Open University of the Netherlands, Herleen NETHERLANDS (e-mail: marcus.specht@ou.nl).

S. Stoyanov is an experienced researcher and consultant in innovative design and evaluation of learning and training at the Open University of the Netherlands, Herleen NETHERLANDS (e-mail: slavi.stoyanov@ou.nl).

Manuscript received 22 March 2018. This work was supported in part by the European Union under Grant 2016-1-DE01-KA203-002915.

Published as submitted by the author(s).

Absence of Decorin Exacerbates DMM-induced Post-traumatic Osteoarthritis in Mice

Qing Li[1], Chao Wang[1], Liu Ouyang[1], Wei Tong[2], Wei-Ju Tseng[2], X. Sherry Liu[2], Renato V. Iozzo[3], Ling Qin[2], David E. Birk[4], Lin Han[1]

[1]School of Biomedical Engineering, Science and Health Systems, Drexel University, Philadelphia, PA, [2]Perelman School of Medicine, University of Pennsylvania, Philadelphia, PA, [3]Jefferson University, Jefferson University, Philadelphia, [4]Morsani College of Medicine, University of South Florida, Tampa

INTRODUCTION: Post-traumatic osteoarthritis (PTOA) is the prevalent form of OA in young adults, while its molecular pathogenesis is not well understood. This study aims to determine the roles of decorin, a critical cartilage extracellular matrix (ECM) molecule, in PTOA. Our recent study discovered that decorin plays an essential role in regulating cartilage assembly and mechanical function of normal cartilage ECM. In early human OA, decorin is markedly up-regulated, suggesting that it is a central participant in OA progression. **METHODS:** Destabilization of the medial meniscus (DMM) surgery was performed on the right hind knees of mature, 12-week-old, male C57BL/6 wild-type (WT) and decorin-null (*Dcn-null*) mice. The Sham control surgery was performed on the contralateral left knees. Mice were euthanized at 8 weeks post-surgery for subsequent studies, including gross-level OA signs via Safranin-O/Fast Green histology and the modified Mankin scoring metrics, cartilage modulus via AFM-nanoindentation, surface collagen fibril structure via SEM and subchondral bone structure (STB) via microCT. **RESULTS:** In WT mice, immunofluorescence demonstrated an up-regulation of decorin after DMM (Fig. 1a), confirming the active involvement of decorin in the DMM OA model. After DMM, *Dcn-null* mice developed more severe OA than the WT, as signified by accelerated sulfated glycosaminoglycans (sGAGs) depletion, higher Mankin OA scores, more pronounced surface fibrillation, reduced cartilage modulus and substantial STB thickening (Fig. 1b-g). **DISCUSSION:** One hallmark of OA is the loss of aggrecan and its associated sGAGs. Our results suggest that decorin is a key regulator of the OA-associated aggrecan loss, which is highlighted by the accelerated sGAGs depletion and modulus reduction in *Dcn-null* cartilage. As a result, *Dcn-null* cartilage also undergoes more pronounced surface fibrillation and subchondral bone thickening, which are resulted from the loss of protection by cartilage aggrecan, and are signs of more advanced OA. Taken together, this study highlights the critical roles of decorin in OA progression, and provides a basis for decorin to serve as a target for potential OA treatment.

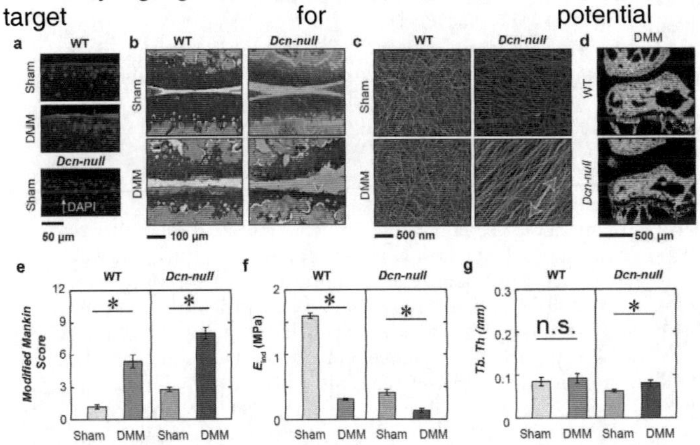

Figure 1 a) Immunofluorescence staining of decorin in murine cartilage shows WT cartilage has increased decorin at 8 weeks after DMM. **b)** Safranin-O/Fast Green histology on cartilage shows the depletion of sGAGs staining and cartilage damage in *Dcn-null* cartilage (red arrow head). **c)** SEM images of cartilage surface fibrils (red arrow: collagen fibrillation along mediolateral direction on *Dcn-null* cartilage surface. **d)** Subchondral trabecular bone frontal plane image via microCT (red square: subchondral trabecular bone thickening). **e)** Modified OA Mankin scores after surgery. **f)** Modulus of medial condyle cartilage after surgery. **g)** Trabecular thickness of subchondral trabecular bone. (*: $p < 0.05$ via wilcoxon signed rank test, mean ± SEM, n ≥ 5 joints each).

Improving the Creation, Curation and Discovery of Open Educational Resources for Work-Integrated and Lifelong Learning

William Jobe[1], Stefan Nilsson[1], Patrik Bernhardsson[1] and Anders Bindslev Rask[2]

[1] University West/Informatics, Trollhättan, Sweden

[2] University College Nordjylland, Aalborg, Denmark

***Abstract*— This paper concerns open education (OER) resources, and more specifically the process of publishing OER material to make it easier to find on the web. The overarching goals are to improve the creation and discovery of OER material for workplace learning as well as strive towards UNESCO's Sustainable Development Goal 4, which aims to ensure inclusive and equitable quality education and promote lifelong learning opportunities for all. As we see it, there are two key challenges. The first challenge regards the content creation and curation side; i.e. the process of making OER material available to the general public, how to maintain the resource and how to get feedback on it. The second challenge regards discovery i.e. for OER consumers to easily find OER material and discern its usefulness in their specific learning context.**

We are in the process of developing a web based system that aids content creators in publishing and maintaining their OER material. The system helps the content creator by generating semantic metadata about the resource based on the Dublin Core system and creates a package of the material itself along with said metadata in a search engine optimized HTML5 file, ready for publishing on a web server or a video streaming site like YouTube, or other media sharing sites.

This approach primarily utilizes common search engines to find the material, thus making the OER material decentralized and not necessarily specific to a specific OER repository. The metadata created by the system does, however, enable developers to create systems specialized in collecting and aggregating OER material, further enhancing the capability of the decentralized ecosystem of OER resources to be used by learning management systems. The key contribution is a suggestion as to how to automatically generate and use an OERID so that all resources can be discovered, curated, and reused.

***Index Terms*—Discoverability, OER, Dublin Core, HTML5**

I. INTRODUCTION

The term OER was first coined at the UNESCO forum in 2002 to refer to the need for a universal educational resource available for all of humanity [1]. Since the inception of this concept, the term OER has come to mean a resource for "teaching, learning and research materials in any medium that reside in the public domain and have been released under an open license that permits access, use, repurposing, reuse, and redistribution by others with no or limited restrictions" [2]. This definition provides the key ingredients of OER, which are that they are for learning and teaching, open and reusable and exist in a variety of mediums. Over the last fifteen years, a variety of private, public and open stakeholders have initiated numerous OER initiatives in the form of portals, databases and repositories [3].

The growth and use of discrete OER repositories has created several problems. Many overlapping and competing standards and educational metadata schemas have been used and proposed overtime, including IEEE LTSC LOM (http://ltsc.ieee.org/wg12/par1484-12-1.html) (Learning Object Metadata), one of the widest adopted, IMS (www.imsglobal.org/metadata/), Ariadne, ISO/IEC MLR - ISO 19788 (www.iso.org/iso/), Metadata for Learning Resources (MLR) and Dublin Core [4]. Furthermore, the web consists of a multitude of platforms that are accessed from a variety of devices and several metadata schemas are used by OER repositories and these repositories offer very heterogeneous datasets, differing with respect to schema, exploited vocabularies, and interface mechanisms [4].

The need to address the issues of heterogeneous standards and schemas is well-known and "accessibility is absolutely vital for a project to produce truly 'open' educational resources" [5]. Previous research presents a few specific issues with OER. Four major challenges for OER according to [4] are integrating distributed data from heterogeneous educational repositories, dealing with continuous change, how to structure texts and evolve taxonomies, and how to compile metadata to facilitate web discovery at scale. According to [6] another current issue with OER is that there is no mobile distribution platform. [7] further mentions the size of the search pool and the ability to filter by resource properties as issues that must be addressed by OER search tools. Finally, [4] point out that web searches of educational resources face a heterogeneous landscape and individual repositories and metadata stores largely use XML and relational databases.

OER is used in several different contexts. One such context is the area of Work-Integrated Learning (WIL). [8] propose how the OER movement can become a key foundation for curating WIL practices which are mindful of disciplinary heritage, local institutional contexts and fostering a capability approach. "The notion of curating work-integrated learning via the OER movement is proposed as a way of not just preserving the past, but also as a way of innovating present and future practices as well" [8].

II. BACKGROUND AND OER RESEARCH OVERVIEW

Some previous research focuses on the use of different metadata systems to tag OER and addresses issues of discovery and curation. The LOM-based search approach is an opportunity for teachers and students to teach and learn together in a collaborative learning environment. The selected fields from the LOM standard enable access to educational resources in different web-based search systems in a formal and effective manner [9]. Linked Data technologies enable the development of the next generation of OER, allowing the separation of semantics from syntax, the improvement of discoverability and access, and the use of common vocabularies, and additionally, the proposed architecture provides an opportunity to merge data distributed across different libraries [10]. The CROERA (Cross-Repository Open Educational Resources Aggregation) system is an aggregator of educational resource repositories that enables access to resources independently of the taxonomy utilized to classify the content in each repository. This enables users accustomed to the descriptions and classification strategy of a particular repository to discover resources in other repositories without needing to switch to another taxonomy or classification scheme. This platform was designed to integrate any existing repository [11].

While the metadata schemes evolve, issues have been raised as to the quality of the metadata as entered by users (see for example [12], [13]. [13] also note that this is an issue that has remained true for an extended time, citing previous research findings reporting that only a fraction of the available fields from various metadata schemes was used to identify and describe an OER.

[5] found that search engine optimization (SEO), meshing existing OER resources with social web functions and recommendation systems are key avenues to explore for OER discoverability. An "appropriate OER" must be understood as a document that at least allows re-purposers to modify contents on both the legal (license) and the technical (format) level [14]. [14] also propose that the possibility to change an OER resource should be mandatory in the metadata, that an OER object comes in both the original, unchangeable format and a reusable format and that all repurposed resources are made public to ensure continuity. Regarding perceptions and attitudes towards OER, [15] found that key areas to address were the need for more information and a need for central repositories that are easily discoverable. Concerning mobile authoring tools for OER creation, [16] presented and tested a mobile application MAAIMS (Mobile Authentic Authoring in IMS) that enabled content creation that was shareable via a repository and reusable in multiple contexts. Finally, [17] concluded that web 2.0 tools improve OER searches by using their semantic meaning. The social and semantic components of the OER production cycle reduces the time needed for development of resources, and including social and semantic components in OER production is without a doubt an opportunity to take advantage of the benefits of web-related trends that provide pertinence, relevance and meaning to the resources.

A. *Creation, Curation and Discovery*

The complexity of the issues for the dissemination and adoption of OER can be reduced to three key issues: creation, curation and discovery. In an OER context creation is the process of creating, tagging, licensing, packaging and sharing an OER object, curation is the process of managing, reusing and adapting an OER resource, and discovery is the process of easily finding an appropriate OER object. [6] describes that there is a lack of curation in the digital content ecosystem. [7] explains that publishers as well as educators consider discovery as a barrier to OER adoption. The same conclusion is presented by [18], listing "No comprehensive catalog" and "Too hard to find what I need" as the two top reasons deterring educators from the use of OER. Furthermore, [7] states that the three key ingredients for an OER discovery tool are curation, indexing and metadata exchange.

One common solution to address OER creation, curation and discovery is to use search engines in combination with existing tools and technologies. The single most important function for metadata is to facilitate resource discovery which in a practical OER context means facilitating a web search [5]. As [19] explain, the use of search engines as a primary tool for discovering academic content should be discussed and addressed, when considering how to increase access to OER. An improved OER search tool should not require the adoption of specific technologies and should leverage the behavior of users, as well as help them refine and filter searches based on metadata as provided by the creator or a curator [7]. Further, a OER discovery tool should provide results that are relevant, usable and from multiple sources [7]. [20] proposes hosting OER in at least two locations to overcome the vulnerability of discrete web repositories, and by using SEO techniques and social media channels, OER can quickly become widely dispersed and discoverable. The ultimate aim is to unify the fragmented landscape for OER on the web [4], [21].

III. RESEARCH AIM

The first challenge regards creation and curation; i.e. the process of making OER material available to the general public and maintaining the resource. The second challenge is discovery; i.e. allow OER consumers to easily find OER material and discern its usefulness in a specific learning context. The aim of this research is to address creation, curation and discovery issues with OER by proposing a simple online tool that automates the process of creating OER objects.

The following sections describe the online tool as a proof of concept to address these longstanding issues with OER.

IV. RESULTS

Much in line with [20], [4] and [21], we propose an OER tool to address the identified issues of creation, curation and discovery by aiding content creators to automatically tag their OER resources relevantly and allowing the creators to host their OER resources on web hosting services or social media services. Research and suggestions from e.g. [5], [19] and [7] support the idea of sharing an OER resource on existing, open platforms that are easily acccssible through search engines and not just specific OER repositories. In order to do so, we suggest an automatically generated OERID as a unique identifier for all OER objects. This OERID can then be used to track curation and simplify the discovery process. The focus on and use of an automatically generated unique OERID further addresses the problem with curation. The OERID will allow for any OER object to be tracked, repurposed and reused throughout the life of the resource and any changes can be logged and tracked as well. Finally, the combination of simplified, automated creation, tagging and publishing of a resource with an OERID directly addresses the three issues of creation, curation, and discovery. Table 1 summarizes how the proposed prototype addresses the aforementioned issues.

A. Prototype description

The prototype presented here is a “proof of concept”, developed with the aim of utilizing it as a tool for

TABLE I.
OER ISSUES AND PROPOSED SOLUTIONS

Issue	Proposed solution from OER tool/prototype
Creation	Simplify and streamline creation and tagging process Automatically generate a unique OERID Allow for publication of the resource on open, social platforms
Curation	The use of a unique OERID allows for a resource to be tracked and thus curated, when reused or repurposed
Discovery	By using a unique OERID and open platforms accessible from common search engines, resources are easier to discover and link to

discovering the feasibility of addressing the aforementioned issues of creation, curation and discovery of OERs using contemporary web technologies. Key considerations for developing the prototype were thus to simplify the process of tagging the OER for the content creator and create metadata about the object in order to aid in the process of publishing a findable, well described OER resource.

Using standard web components, the prototype is driven on the backend by Node.js together with several open source JavaScript components allowing for the extraction of metadata about the OER object to automate the tagging process as much as possible. A few open web technologies are used on the frontend, predominantly Angular.js providing the user interface and JavaScript components allowing for the upload of files.

B. Describing the OER

To mark up the OER material, the content creator has to fill in a number of metadata fields describing the material. As previously stated, several metadata schemes for marking up the OER metadata exists, using more or less extensive and exhaustive sets of fields for the author to fill in. Although extensive, previous research has reported that the quality of the metadata on existing OERs within repositories is low, suggesting that there is a need to aid the content creator as much as possible in the process of describing the material.

Logging in using the content creator’s email address, the user is presented with the opportunity to upload the OER material (see Fig. 1). The upload feature is mainly used to extract the metadata from the material. At present, the prototype supports the most common image types, video files (in the form of mp4) and documents in the form of PDFs.

Figure 1. The OERID user interface

After the file has been uploaded, the user can fill in the fields from the Dublin Core Metadata Element Set standard [22]. Depending on the amount of metadata that has been extracted from the file at upload, some of the fields are prefilled. The user can adjust these fields in case they are inaccurate. Table 2 outlines the fields according to the Dublin Core Metadata Element Set, and demarks fields that can a) be automatically filled in, or b) be suggested by extracting data from the web server, the user’s browser or the resource’s metadata. Further, the prototype can be personalized in such way that the user can add common contributors, coverage, publisher, and subject to be reused.

TABLE II.
OER ISSUES AND PROPOSED SOLUTIONS

Term	Short Description	Automated
Contributor	Name of person contribution to the resource	Suggested
Coverage	Names of places and dates the resource covers	Suggested
Creator	Name of the creator of the resource	Suggested
Date	A date of the resource	Yes
Description	A text describing the resource	No
Format	The file format or distribution form. Could also be dimensions of an image or duration of a video.	Yes
Identifier	A unique reference to the resource	Yes (**OERID**)
Language	The language associated with the resource	Suggested
Publisher	Name of organization or person publishing the resource	Suggested
Relation	ID of a related resource, could be an OERID	No
Rights	Property rights associated with the resource	Suggested
Source	Identity of a resource from which this resource is derived, could be an OERID	No
Subject	The overarching topic of the resource using keywords	Suggested
Title	The formal name of the resource	No
Type	Type of resource, such as "image" or "text"	Yes

An OERID is automatically generated for the file, tying together the user with a particular OER resource. The unique OERID is an alphanumeric string generated by the application as a MD5 hash using the user's e-mail address, the filename and file size of the resource, the type of the resource, together with a timestamp from the server at the time of upload. Finally, the alphanumeric string is prepended with the string "OERID". As such, the OERID can be used to validate the origin of the material. In extension, the OERID can also be used as a resource identifier by other services such as specialized OER search engines as well as for example curation and validation services.

C. Distribution of the OER

When the necessary fields are completed, the user submits the form. The system then generates a package of files for the user to download. The package contains an HTML5 document using semantic tags containing the metadata of the OER, as well as a link to the OER object itself. Creating a semantic HTML5 document helps with the SEO as well as the presentation of the resource itself. Using the files in the package, the content creator is able to distribute the material to a web location of their choice. In the case that the OER is a video, the content creator can further use any video sharing service such as YouTube or Vimeo, and provide the unique OERID in the description.

D. Curation of OER

Using the OERID, collections of open educational resources can be curated by web services. Utilizing the OERID both as an identifier of a resource as well as using it as an identifier of a related resource and a resource from which it is a derivative of, one can track a single OER and how it relates to other OERs.

V. DISCUSSION

This paper has explored current issues relating to the use of OER, and identified three areas of interest: the creation, curation and discovery of OER material. A key discussion question is how to alleviate these issues. As [20] states "We will need to consider whether we wish to continue tracking the fate of our content, or whether those involved in global open education will have to accept that OER will fledge and leave their project nests as part of the natural cycle of events." Our proposed prototype eases creation and uses a unique OERID that offers a solution for curation and discovery. The prototype encourages OER content creators to share their OER resources on a variety of platforms, thus freeing the material from closed repositories. However, our suggested solution still allows for creators to track and make the material easily accessible from a general search engine by using an OERID together with a semantic HTML in a HTML5 format. We view this solution as the best of both worlds, i.e. OER material can be shared anywhere and easily found without losing the ability to track and curate the material.

Another issue of discussion is the use of OER resources in different contexts. There are several contexts such as e.g. work-integrated learning, lifelong learning (non-formal education), formal education and open education for fulfilling UNESCO's SDG goals, where research highlights the need for better utilization of OER resources and the possible benefits of increased OER use. Our proposed prototype has the potential to make headway in these contexts by increasing the discoverability and availability of OER resources. Furthermore, the ability to track, curate and repurpose OER resources using the OERID can allow for the development of informal communities in these contexts that can lead to increased quantity and quality of OER resources.

The concept of using a unique ID, the proposed OERID, for tracking all OER resources has both advantages, disadvantages and technical issues. A key advantage of the OERID is that it provides a way to uniquely identify and track an OER resource for the life of the resource. This is advantageous as it provides improved discoverability and curation. Another advantage is that the ability to track changes to an original resource provides transparency to any changes and repurposing. We also see the possibility for content creators to trace an OER to see where and in which contexts a specific resource they created is being used. This can also be used as a validation tool for teachers and educators looking for OER material, seeing where and by whom a resource has previously been used.

However, a possible disadvantage of the OERID is that it can decrease anonymity of a resource that can be desirable in certain contexts. Furthermore, there are some technical issues regarding format and "uniqueness" of the

OERID. Our prototype is a proof of concept and the algorithm used to create the OERID should be analyzed and discussed in more detail. We deem our proposed algorithm that automatically generates the OERID to be unique enough, but will it scale if use increases drastically? Would it be better to strictly create the OERID from exif data from a resource and randomly generated string without requiring user data (email in our algorithm)?

While the prototype automates certain aspects of describing an OER according to the Dublin Core Metadata Element Set standard [22], the results vary depending on the type and format of the resource. As the automation of describing the OER lowers, we expect that the quality of metadata follows the same pattern. One can argue that since the idea of this project is to allow for OERs to be publicly available on standard web services and trackable by the OERID, it could provide a breeding ground for applications and services further aiding the creation, curation and discoverability of OERs. One such application could be what [12] term collaborative metadata creation, where the content creators can gain assistance from metadata specialists as well as users in the OER community in improving the metadata quality.

VI. Concluding Remarks

The aim of this paper has been to explore how, by the use of technology, we can alleviate the hurdles of creating, curating and discovering OER material. The prototype developed aids the content creator in the creation stage by automating the process of filling in the fields from the Dublin Core Metadata Element Set standard [22]. Further, it creates a unique identifier for each OER resource, dubbed the OERID, assisting content owners in the curation of the resource they have provided the OER community. When it comes to the discovery stage, the application creates a standardized HTML5 file that accompanies the OER resource. Utilizing semantic tagging of the provided DCME fields helps search providers such as Google and Bing to find and rank the OER material. The OERID can also be used in the description field of video streaming sites such as YouTube or Vimeo to identify the resource.

References

[1] UNESCO. (2002). Forum on the impact of open courseware for higher education in developing countries (pp. 1–30). Retrieved from http://portal.unesco.org/ci/en/ev.php-URL_ID=2492&URL_DO=DO_TOPIC&URL_SECTION=201.html

[2] Atkins, D. E., Brown, J. S., & Hammond, A. L. (2007). A review of the Open Educational Resources (OER) movement: Achievements, challenges, and new opportunities, 1–84.

[3] Wang, T., & Towey, D. (2017). Open educational resource (OER) adoption in higher education: Challenges and strategies (pp. 317–319). IEEE. https://doi.org/10.1109/TALE.2017.8252355

[4] Dietze, S., Sanchez-Alonso, S., Ebner, H., Qing Yu, H., Giordano, D., Marenzi, I., & Pereira Nunes, B. (2013). Interlinking educational resources and the web of data: A survey of challenges and approaches. Program, 47(1), 60–91. https://doi.org/10.1108/00330331211296312

[5] Thomas, A., Campbell, L. M., Barker, P., & Hawksey, M. (Eds.) (2012). Into the wild – Technology for open educational resources. University of Bolton.

[6] St. Lifer, E. (2018). Five Ed-Tech Elephants: From OER to equitable access, challenges to the digital revolution persist. School Library Journal, (1), 12.

[7] Yergler, N. R. (2010). Search and Discovery : OER's Open Loop. Retrieved from http://openaccess.uoc.edu/webapps/o2/handle/10609/4852

[8] Simpson, M. D., & Twist, T. (2016). Curating Work-Integrated Learning: "Taking Care" of Disciplinary Heritage, Local Institutional Contexts and Wellbeing via the Open Educational Resources Movement. Asia-Pacific Journal of Cooperative Education, 17(1), 1–8.

[9] Valiente, M.-C., Sicilia, M.-A., Garcia-Barriocanal, E., & Rajabi, E. (2015). Adopting the metadata approach to improve the search and analysis of educational resources for online learning. Computers in Human Behavior, 51, 1134–1141. https://doi.org/10.1016/j.chb.2014.12.059

[10] Piedra, N., Chicaiza, J. A., López, J., & Tovar, E. (2014). An Architecture based on Linked Data technologies for the Integration and reuse of OER in MOOCs Context. Open Praxis, 6(2). https://doi.org/10.5944/openpraxis.6.2.122

[11] Mouriño-García, M., Pérez-Rodríguez, R., Anido-Rifón, L., Fernández-Iglesias, M. J., & Darriba-Bilbao, V. M. (2018). Cross-repository aggregation of educational resources. Computers & Education, 117, 31–49. https://doi.org/10.1016/j.compedu.2017.09.014

[12] Currier, S., Barton, J., O'Beirne, R., & Ryan, B. (2004). Quality assurance for digital learning object repositories: issues for the metadata creation process. ALT-J, Research in Learning Technology, 12(1).

[13] Palavitsinis, N., Manouselis, N., & Sanchez-Alonso, S. (2014). Metadata quality in learning object repositories: a case study. The Electronic Library, 32(1), 62-82.

[14] Richter, T., & Veith, P. (2014). Fostering the Exploitation of Open Educational Resources. Open Praxis, 6(3). https://doi.org/10.5944/openpraxis.6.3.139

[15] Belikov, O. M., & Bodily, R. (2016). Incentives and Barriers to OER Adoption: A Qualitative Analysis of Faculty Perceptions. Open Praxis, 8(3), 235–246.

[16] Kinshuk, D., & Jesse, R. (2013). Mobile authoring of open educational resources as reusable learning objects. The International Review of Research in Open and Distributed Learning, 14(2), 28. https://doi.org/10.19173/irrodl.v14i2.1535

[17] Carrion, C., Patricia, S., Morales, R., del Rocio, G., Pelaez, R., & Elizabeth, A. (2010). OER's production cycle with social authorship and semantic tools (pp. 121–128). IEEE. https://doi.org/10.1109/EDUCON.2010.5492588

[18] Allen, I. E., & Seaman, J. (2014). Opening the Curriculum: Open Educational Resources in US Higher Education, 2014. Babson Survey Research Group.

[19] Ladbrook, J., & Prober, E. (2011). Information Skills and Critical Literacy: Where Are Our Digikids at with Online Searching and Are Their Teachers Helping? Australasian Journal of Educational Technology, 27(1), 105–121.

[20] Rolfe, V. (2016). Web Strategies for the Curation and Discovery of Open Educational Resources. Open Praxis, 8(4), 297–312. https://doi.org/10.5944/openpraxis.8.4.305

[21] Chicaiza, J., Piedra, N., Lopez-Vargas, J., & Tovar-Caro, E. (2014). Domain Categorization of Open Educational Resources Based on Linked Data. In Knowledge Engineering and the Semantic Web (pp. 15–28). Springer, Cham. https://doi.org/10.1007/978-3-319-11716-4_2

[22] Dublincore.org (2012). Dublin Core Metadata Element Set, Version 1.1: Reference Description. [ONLINE] Available at: http://dublincore.org/documents/dces/. [Accessed 13 March 2018]

Authors

First Author W. Jobe, is with University West in Trollhättan, Sweden. He is now with the Department of Informatics, (e-mail: william.jobe@hv.se).

Second Author S. Nilsson is with University West in Trollhättan, Sweden. He is with the department of Informatics, School of Media and Design (e-mail: stefan.nilsson@hv.se).

Third Author P. Bernhardsson is with University West in Trollhättan, Sweden. He is now with the Department of Informatics, where he works as a lecturer in digital media, focusing on web development (e-mail: patrik.bernhardsson@hv.se).

Fourth Author A. Bindslev Rask is with University College Nordjylland, Aalborg, Denmark (e-mail: andr@ucn.dk)

Manuscript received 25 May 2018.

Published as submitted by the author(s).

An Accessible Model House for Demonstrating an Independent Living Environment

Alexis Welch[1], Ahmaad Randall[1], Amy Harmon[1], Ying Sun, Ph.D. [1]
[1]Biomedical Engineering, University of Rhode Island, Kingston, RI

Background: Although many assistive devices (AD) for daily living exist, lack of public awareness of ADs and limited modes of AD orientation hinder the ability of disabled individuals to make fully educated decisions on a solution that meets their needs. The conventional alternatives of facilities and personal care professionals commonly lower sense of independence and quality of life. This project aims to provide a mode of introducing available ADs and exhibit how they can be operated in a patient's home. **Method**: A two-story home with a kitchen storage assembly was modeled using a scaled-down, 3-dimensional house made from foam board. This model was created to demonstrate how an automated wheelchair lift and light switch system can be integrated into a standard home design. The development of this model involved the design of an Android application, light switch and motor control circuitry designs a wheelchair lift, and a motor driven pulley system. A microprocessor was used to allow remote control of the light switch and wheelchair lift using an Android tablet in order for the Android device application to wirelessly control the systems. **Results**: The figure displays a schematic of the model house and a diagram of the system components to demonstrate how the architectural, physical, and electrical design specifications accurately represent a realistic house adapted for assistive living. The diagram of the shelf-lowering countertop displays the physical design specifications and functionality of an adapted storage and countertop option. In addition to the design specifications of each component of the model, the pulley system assembly diagram demonstrates how the wheelchair lift is mechanically operated and electrically controlled. **Conclusion**: These technologies have the potential to allow individuals living in an assisted living facilities to be able to transition to their own private home, or individuals already living in their own home to have a reduced need for a personal care professional. The Model House provides a visual and interactive example of the different ways in which individuals with disabilities can use technology to adapt a conventionally-built home into an independent living environment.

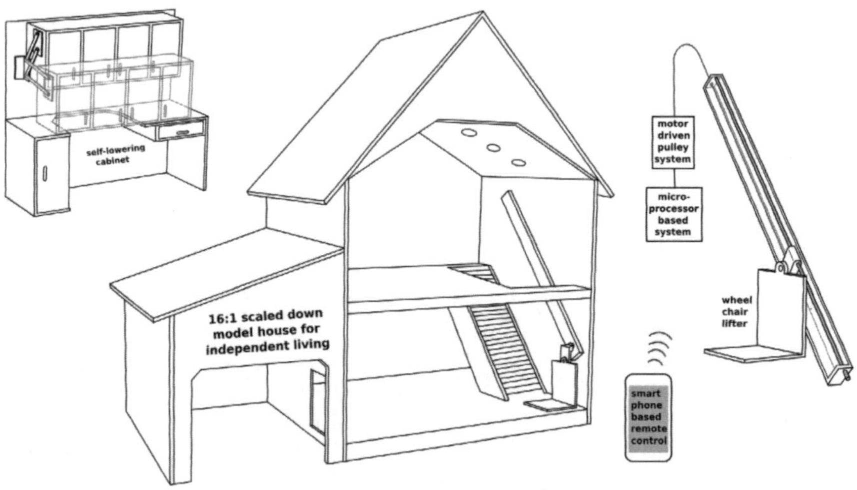

Working in increasing isolation? How an international MOOC for career professionals supports peer learning across distance

Barbara Kieslinger[1], Juliet Tschank[2], Teresa Schäfer[1], and Claudia Magdalena Fabian[1]

[1] Centre for Social Innovation GmbH (ZSI)/Technology & Knowledge (T&W), Vienna, Austria

[2] Centre for Social Innovation GmbH (ZSI)/Work & Equal Opportunities (A&C), Vienna, Austria

Abstract— **In this contribution we provide an assessment of an international MOOC that was designed specifically for professionals in employment services and career guidance. The six-week course was implemented in the context of a wider spanning project on the study of professional identity transformations and was building on the experience of smaller courses provided in closed organizational settings. By opening up the course and transferring it into a MOOC format, almost 90 professionals from around 20 countries were able to share their work experiences and discuss challenges in their daily work related to demographic change, digitalization and organizational change. Amongst the most active contributors were those participants, who were confronted with an increasing isolation at work: being either placed in remote areas, part of a distributed team or a "functional" island. For them, learning from and with others as part of an online community, becomes increasingly important, as reflected by the participants' feedback and their comments during the course. The analysis clearly stresses the importance of the exchange of experiences with colleagues and peers. While tutor input was also appreciated, participants especially appreciate the learning from their peers. A MOOC or online community can serve an important role in collaborative reflection and social learning. Given this experience, MOOCs could be offered specifically for certain professions where people work in isolation, either in geographical terms or in terms of the topics they are covering.**

Index Terms—**MOOC, peer learning, social learning, workplace learning.**

I. Introduction

Approximately five years ago, an international research team set out to facilitate the learning processes of career guidance professionals, who are challenged enormously in their service delivery due to demographic change, rising unemployment, digitalization and a series of other global factors changing the world of work. A main hypothesis of this research team, which worked within the framework of the EmployID[1] project, funded by the European Union, was that career professionals, and especially those working in public employment services (PES), are constantly undergoing a transformation process of their professional identity, which can be seen as a learning and personal development process that can be supported by appropriate means of facilitation [1].

After three years of experimentation and piloting in different organizational settings [2], the gained experiences were transferred into an open learning environment in the form of a MOOC (Massive Open Online Courses). The aim of this online learning was to address the most important aspects of the changing world of work, to discuss how these changes affect career guidance professionals and to present them with tools and strategies on how to deal with these challenges in a professional workplace setting.

In this paper, the feedback and experiences from the almost 90 international participants of this online learning will be presented and discussed. Interestingly, comments from some of the most active participants revealed that these individuals were working in some sort of remote setting and under a certain feeling of isolation. The following analysis will thus focus on the social and peer learning aspects that the participants experienced in the framework of the learning platform.

II. Social Workplace Learning

Informal workplace learning is often closely related to the concept of social learning. The idea of social learning is that people learn through observing others behavior, attitudes and outcomes of these behaviors, and apply this in future actions of their own [3]. Social learning takes place in the interaction with other colleagues and peers, in groups, teams and networks. With the growing digitalization of workplaces and the use of ICT, social learning is increasingly taking place in digitally mediated settings, such as eLearning portals or social networking platforms.

In recent years, MOOCs, which originally emerged in higher education, have also started to enter workplace learning. They are considered as a promising approach to augmenting, scaling, and redefining training and making it more cost-effective. Broadly speaking, MOOCs are categorized as either xMOOCs or cMOOCs, where xMOOCs rely on content delivery and cMOOCs are designed as collaborative platforms for learner engagement and making use of the social networking ecology. cMOOCs have thus been considered as social learning spaces characterized by aspects such as sharing and communication of knowledge and experiences, building on existing knowledge, collaboration and social, support, etc. [4].

The growing importance of permanent informal social learning as an answer to permanent change processes at work has been stressed by recent workplace learning studies. Gil and Mataveli's [5] analysis of the impact of

[1] https://employid.eu/

organizational learning culture and learning facilitators in workplace group learning concludes that organizational commitment to the development of informal learning is crucial. In such informal workplace learning settings MOOCs have the potential to support both professional development and lifelong learning [6].

III. Towards More Self-Management at Work

New forms of increasingly flexible working models are an important consequence of digitalization. These new ways of working may bring advantages to employers and employees alike, in the form of improved work-life balance, autonomy and flexibility of working from home [7]. However, higher flexibility can also result in higher income uncertainty, higher responsibility for one's own education and training and a transfer of risks from employer to the employee (or self-employed contractor) [7].

Another consequence of the changing work models is an increasing social isolation of dispersed workers and self-employed contractors, which again stresses the growing importance of digitally mediated settings of social learning. Social isolation increases by the amount of time spent working remotely and decreases through face-to-face interactions and access to communication technology [8]. However, social isolation not only concerns those working from home, but also those working isolated in their organization in mainly virtual tasks with colleagues from other locations [9]. Practical guidelines found on the Internet suggest concrete measures of counteracting social isolation when working in remote settings. Creating online networks with professional contacts tends to be a common recommendation.[2] Informal online learning platforms, such as MOOCs, can provide self-managed workers a space for their social interaction.

IV. Method

A. Hypothesis

This paper aims to reveal the general perceptions of learners participating in an international MOOC in terms of personal gains. A main hypothesis when implementing this course was that online social learning can contribute to supporting professional development of individuals, not only by consuming the provided content, but more importantly via the engagement with other learners. In other words, the hypothesis was that social online learning, especially in the framework of cMOOCs, where the focus is on exchange of experiences among participants, can support remote workers in their challenges to adjust their work practice. In addition, as the empirical data are mostly based on feedback questionnaires, this paper will also discuss some learner preferences with regards to the specific content units and their general learning experiences.

B. Study context: cMOOC course design

This paper presents the results of the online learning course delivered on the European Multiple MOOC Aggregator (EMMA) platform[3] titled: "The Changing World of Work"[4] (see Figure 1). This course was free of charge and open to all regardless of geographical location and occupational field. However, it is worth noting that due to its very specialized content, the MOOC addressed a specific group of people, namely persons involved in job placement be it employees of PES, guidance practitioners, job coaches etc.

The content of the MOOC was divided into five main topics delivered over six weeks. As the idea of a MOOC is to learn at one's own pace according to one's own time resources, the content was available for a total of three months; from March to June 2017. At the same time the course design placed a lot of importance on peer-to-peer learning as demonstrated by its so called "core principles", which stressed the engagement in discussions, sharing of thoughts and ideas and reflections on personal experiences and learnings[4]. The interaction between participants was facilitated by eight tutors, who initiated discussion threads, encouraged commenting on specific paragraphs of the content and engaged in social media (e.g. on Twitter with the hashtag #EmployIDMOOC).

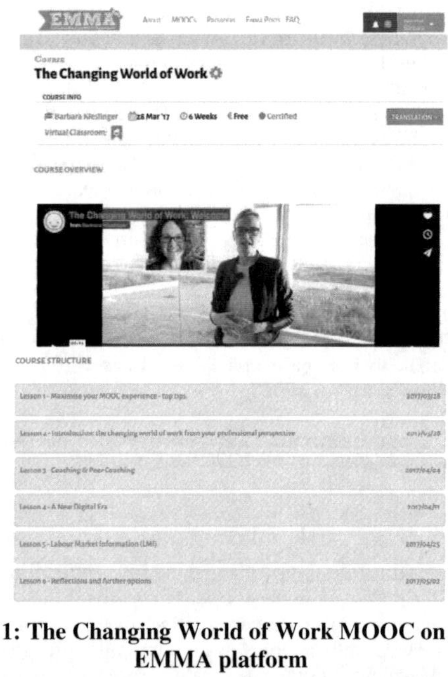

Fig. 1: The Changing World of Work MOOC on the EMMA platform

The five content topics included: A "Professional Perspective [of the changing world of work]", "an introduction to Coaching and Peer Coaching", "a New Digital Era", "Labor Market Information (LMI)" and "Reflective Practice" [10]. Learners were eased into the online course by getting to understand how the world of work is changing for example through technology or

[2] https://www.theguardian.com/small-business-network/2017/may/10/home-alone-dealing-with-the-solitude-of-self-employment or http://www.myrkothum.com/self-employed-isolation/

[3] https://platform.europeanmoocs.eu/

[4] https://platform.europeanmoocs.eu/course_the_changing_world_of_work

globalization and how they can best embrace this challenge to succeed. Following this, they were provided with tools and taught new skills to support their colleagues and clients in stressful situations or in problem-solving through the coaching and peer coaching approach. The learners then tackled the concept of "digital literacy" and specifically looked at how ICT developments, artificial intelligence and the use of open source data are changing the behavior in the workplace. Next, the learners were taught how to go beyond just giving advice to job seekers but rather integrating labor market information and labor market intelligence into their work practice. Finally, in the last week, the learners encountered different tools and techniques to reflect on their experiences in individual and group situations.

The course content was provided in different formats such as videos, texts and links to external resources and was only available in English.

C. *Study design*

The study implemented a one group posttest design [11]. This involves the measurement of the participant group at the end of an intervention. Drawing inference or establish causality as is sometimes suggested in the literature [11] was not intended. Rather, the questionnaire was complemented with a qualitative analysis of comments made by the participants on the MOOC portal. In this case, the intervention was the "Changing World of Work" MOOC course. And the participant group included the learners who filled in the questionnaire at the end of the MOOC for the descriptive statistics and all active learners for the complementary content coding.

D. *Participants*

The participants of the study involved all the participants who vigorously participated in the MOOC and focused especially on the respondents of the questionnaire at the end of the MOOC. From a total of 402 registered participants, 86 actively took part in the MOOC out of which 32 or 37% completed the questionnaire, whereby 30 entries were complete.

Socio-demographic data such as age, gender, country of residence were not collected in the survey and as a result, it is not possible to categorize the participant group into subgroups based on such characteristics. The only variable that allowed some insight into the respondents' characteristics was their professional profile (Fig. 2).

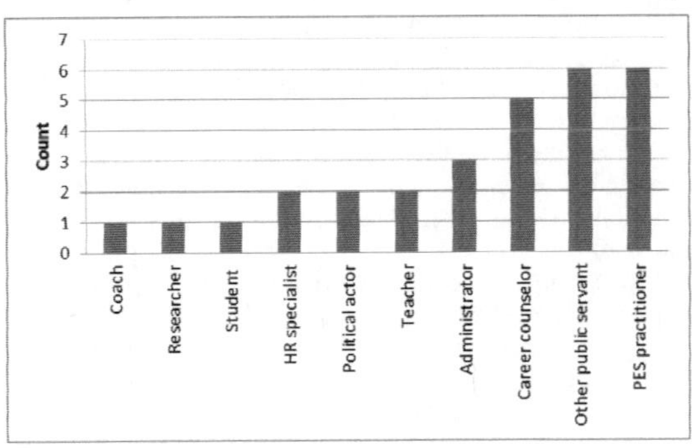

Fig. 2: Respondents' professional profiles

Six participants each, indicated that they are PES practitioners or public servants; five are career counsellors (one who is a senior careers practitioner incorporating elements of research and training); three are administrators (one dealing with the unemployed, a business administrator and a general administrator); two each, are human resource (HR) specialists, teachers or political actors (one, a "think tank on future work" and the other "European employment services adviser") and one participant each, is a researcher, coach or student of career management.

E. *Procedure*

The survey took the form of a self-administered questionnaire [12]. After completing all the modules in the MOOC, the participants were provided with a link to the feedback questionnaire. The questionnaire included 22 closed and four open items.

The closed items of the questionnaire related to five main topics: The content, participation, learning, application of the learning at the workplace and general satisfaction with the course. The items forming the subject of content also covered the course design and delivery. The level of the respondents' personal participation in the course as well as their exchange with other participants was mirrored under the topic of participation. In order to gauge whether the knowledge of the participation in relation to the five content-related modules of the MOOC (changing world of work, coaching and peer coaching, digital agenda, labor market information and reflection) increased as a result of the course, the respondents' level of agreement to six positively formulated items was requested e.g. "I have learnt something important about the Changing World of Work" through this course". The questions representing this topic in particular, attempted to overcome one of the main weaknesses posed by the one group posttest design implemented in this study, the difficulty in establishing causality [13], by asking whether the changes observed, if any, were directly related to the course. This topic was also boosted by one of the open questions requesting for a specific example of course content that influenced the respondents' professional development. What counts even more than just gaining knowledge, is being able to use this knowledge in practice. Following this thought, the course evaluation questionnaire also inquired whether the knowledge that was gained, as covered by the previous topic, learning, could not only be applied in one's professional career development, but also whether the participants felt confident enough with this knowledge to transfer it to others. Finally, two of the closed survey questions examined the overall contentment with the course as a whole. Three of the four open questions also greatly informed this topic: What the participants enjoyed best, what aspects of the course could be improved and other comments.

With regard to the closed items, the participants' degree of agreement to the all the statements except one: "How likely is it that you would recommend the course on 'Changing World of Work' to others?" (statement 17 in Table I below) were provided on a 7-point Likert scale of 0 to 6, whereby 0 represented "does not apply at all" and 6 "applies fully". The one exception required the participants to present their level of agreement to the statement on a 11-point Likert scale of 0 to 10; where 0 represented "not at all" and 10 "very likely".

F. Methods of analysis

Descriptive statistics and exploratory data analysis were carried out on the closed items of the questionnaire [13]. The following measures of central tendency for each of the closed statements are presented in the table below: The arithmetic mean, median and mode. For the open questions in the survey, a conventional [14] or inductive [15] content analysis approach was used.

In addition, the insights gained from the survey were complemented with qualitative data generated from the course participants' contributions during their learning experiences. The available discussions from the course were extracted from the learning platform and analysed by means of qualitative deductive content coding [15] using the software MAXQDA[5]. This qualitative analysis was a complementary step to enrich the feedback from the questionnaire with evidence from the comments learners left directly on the platform. The approach is deductive in the sense that the two coders scanned the material specifically for indications of community building and social interaction during the learning process. Whenever a learner comment from the MOOC discussions is quoted below, reference is given to the unique user ID assigned to each of the MOOC participants.

V. Discussion of Results

The column "topic" in Table I below shows how the questionnaire items were grouped into the five emerging topics.

It is clear that the results of the survey are overall positive with all the means, medians and modes falling on the positive ends of the scale for the 7-point scaled items, four or above and for the 11-point scaled item six and above. In the following section we discuss the five emerging topics from the survey, complemented with learners' statements from the qualitative content coding of the course discussions on the MOOC platform.

A. Content

There was a general consensus by the course participants that the objectives of the course were clear (item 1) and that the content itself was delivered in a comprehensible manner (item 4). This result is strengthened by some comments under one of the open questions where the respondents acknowledged that the course was "*complex*" with "*saturated material*", however at the same time, they appreciated that the course was organised in a "*very systematic*" manner.

The respondents also generally agreed that the course provided both theoretical (item 2) and practical (item 3) knowledge and competences. Under the open question, concerning what they liked best about the course, a number of respondents of the survey also mentioned specific content and delivery format of the content. The provision of the course content in different formats like (short) texts, "*very structured and very explanatory*" videos and extra resources and links for further reading was valued by the participants. Nevertheless, some participants observed that the content was "*heavy on text*" and suggested presenting e-books as videos which were generally considered an asset of the course: "*Maybe those e-books could have been shortened and presented as a video, so anyone who wants can read the whole volume, or just skip it but again have the most important highlights of it*" (sic). Some also suggested making the video content longer, which was often described and to some extent valued by the participants as "*short videos*."

Although there was general agreement that the content was distributed optimally over the course duration (item 6), of all the questionnaire items, this was the item with the lowest mean (M=4.28). This result is also reflected in the answers to the open question: "What needs to be improved?" Here, some participants distinctly mentioned that the content could have been distributed better over the lifespan of the course because time was "*too short on some [specific] units*" or otherwise said "*it takes longer for some of the modules to be completed*."

B. Learning

There was a general agreement that the respondents learnt what they were intended to learn through the online course. This was demonstrated by the fact that 86.7% (items 10 and 22) to 96.7% (item 11) of the respondents rated each item related to learning with a 4 or above. All items achieved a median and mode of 5 except the item: "I have learned something important about labour market information through this course" (item 12) which had a mode of 6.

Supplementary to item 22: "The course has helped me reflect upon my own professional identity," the respondents were required, through an open question, to give examples of specific content or discussions that influenced their professional development. "*Coaching*" which was delivered in week two of the training course, received the most mentions and was found particularly interesting. Many respondents mentioned that they specifically enjoyed, learnt about, and got a "*new mind-set*" on "*peer coaching*". One respondent specified the "*career coaching*" aspects of the unit. As an example of the participants' enthusiasm about this unit, one respondent said: "*I see the peer coaching model to be something I could work with in my department outside my own team if the opportunity arises. In times of flux and change it is very important to have a growth mind-set and to remain resilient this unit was interesting*."

Both the unit on "a new digital era" and the one on "labour market information (LMI)" received the second highest number of mentions as having influenced the way the participants of the course, who completed the questionnaire, see their professional development. The first module on the introduction to the changing world of work as well as the last module on reflection and evaluation received only about half the number of mentions of the other three modules mentioned above; most of which did not have further description. One participant mentioned that the first module enabled him or her to become "*an expert in how the world of work is changing, and helping clients to prepare for the challenges, changes and new skills needed in the future*."

Most of the respondents who mentioned the last module on "reflective practice" as an influencer of their own professional development, also mentioned specific tips and tricks that they learnt from the module; for example,

[5] https://www.maxqda.com/

"*reflection tools and techniques outlined on what to concentrate in writing a proposal or develop activities among unemployed persons when preparing a project*", the "*reflection journal and tips on how to use it*" and even a book recommendation. From all the participants, only one indicated that the course did not have a big enough impact to influence their professional development. He or she mentioned that the lack of time and a learning diary as having contributed to the less than ideal learning experience. Nevertheless, this respondent notes that he or she was able to take away many practical tips and materials from the course.

Amongst the participants' comments on the platform 150 entries relate to the course content. Respondents provided feedback to every week, highlighted specific content features or explained how the content links to their own experiences and learning. One learner stated that "*This lesson [referring to the coaching and peer coaching unit] was great! I am trained coach and principles of coaching are familiar for me. I especially liked the tips for effective behavior for difficult persons. I will use these tips in my daily work! All the material of this lesson should be included to the basic induction for all career counselling professionals* (MOOC-discussion F521CFFC)." Another comment related to digital change: "*This module has taught me the importance of keeping up with the changes in technology by upskilling ourselves through online courses etc.*" (MOOC-discussion A2936C91)." Another comment in week 1 highlights the potential feeling of isolation that some participants shared "*There is a lot in this session! Interesting to reflect on personal learning styles as being quite isolated both geographically and in the workplace have to rely on practitioner groups and other external contacts for advice and guidance* (MOOC-discussion D5CC8CBE)."

C. Application

In workplace learning it is generally the intention that the taught material is useful in one way or the other. In the case of the changing world of work MOOC, almost half of the participants (46.7% or n=14) fully agreed that they can apply the learning from this course on their own professional career development (item 14) by giving it the maximum rating of 6. This coincided with the mode of the item also being 6. Most of the rest of the participants rated the item with a 4 or above – on the positive range (43.3%), while one participant neither agreed nor disagreed with the statement (with a rating of 3) and two assessed the item with a 2; which is tending towards the negative direction, but it is the lowest possible negative value.

With regards to whether the participants of the course were confident about imparting the knowledge gained on others (item 15), all the participants rated the item with a 4 or above, suggesting that they were all confident in fulfilling this expectation.

D. Participation

Regarding participation options during the course, most respondents acknowledged that the learning was organized in a way that it provided them with sufficient opportunity to contribute through asking questions and bringing in their own interests (item 5). Additionally, there was a consensus that enough attention was given to reflection and exchange with other participants (item 7). As far as the intensity of their own personal involvement in the course is concerned, survey respondents were more critical. This is evident from the fact that this statement observed the second lowest mean (M=4.42) and the only that had a median and mode of 4, the lowest of all the items of the questionnaire, nevertheless, still on the positive side of the scale.

The aspect of participation in the course featured prominently in the answers to the open question: "What did you like best." As previously mentioned, the course placed a high significance on learner and tutor interactions. This was one of the elements of the course that were mostly valued by the participants. As an example, one respondent said: "*I liked that we had the opportunity to share ideas with others and I was always excited to read reflections of other participants*." In some cases, where participants did not explicitly mention that they enjoyed taking part in the discussions, they still mentioned that they enjoyed "*learning and reading other peoples' opinions in discussion boxes*." The presence of the tutors in these discussions was also seen as an added value as explained by one of the respondents: "*I liked the opportunity to share thoughts at the end of each unit and was impressed by the way that the team responded to these comments with their thoughts and further information*." The blogs and comments from tutors and their '*constant presence*' in the learning environment were further commended because they [the tutors] "*outlined the essence of each unit*" by highlighting the most important lessons.

Another element of the peer-to-peer learning that was highly valued by the participants was the fact that, as not only the Employ-ID project is international, the course itself was open to all and as a result, was not inhibited by territorial boundaries and even dubbed an "*international course*" by one of the participants. As a consequence of this, different practitioners from all over the world, who would have otherwise probably never come into personal contact, were brought together or became "*virtually acquainted*" as described by one participant, through the course. This enabled the participants to "*hear from international colleagues*' and '*see how employment services in other countries are working*" a phenomenon that they found quite "*satisfying*" and "*curiosity*" arousing.

Although the element of peer-to-peer learning was a by-product of the course rather than being a topic actively injected into the course, it ran along many of the answers to the different open questions. As a result, it also emerged under the open question: "Can you give an example of a content or discussion unit that influenced the way you see your own professional development?" One participant appreciated the opportunity that the course provided to communicate with their colleagues, an aspect that they hold dear, but unfortunately "*in real life it is so difficult to create such dialogues with [other] persons*." For another participant comments from other participants showed them that in similar work environments, the same techniques in working with the unemployed and in developing one's professional skills are used.

The perceived importance of the community was also reflected in the participants' comments on the platform. In more than 100 statements learners appreciated the contributions of their peers and highlighted the effect of these discussions in their learning. "*I am finding the posts of other participants extremely informative and supportive in developing my understanding, and am using it as a form of peer coaching. Thank you* (MOOC-discussion 9B8C8BEA)." The comments highlight what was also reflected in the questionnaires, namely that the exchange across countries and the resulting understanding that practitioners find themselves in similar situations and can and should therefore exchange best practice was perceived as highly valuable for one's own learning. "*I really enjoyed the fact that a lot of people live on my own experiences, and sometimes my own disappointments. There is no difference between one country and another - it seems to me that the world is all the same* (MOOC-discussion 02FCC076)."

However, there were also 16 comments that related to the increasing isolation of career practitioners caused by digitalization. "*Feeling like an island*" was experienced due to functional or geographical isolation and stresses the importance of social online learning with peers at distance even more. A statement to confirm this was: *"I share the feeling of growing distance totally. Most of my colleagues are situated all over Finland in different cities and we communicate using Skype. It's easy to reach people around the country but on the other hand, we almost never see face-to-face because Skype is cheaper. The same goes for my students. Even the colleagues in the same city work from home for a few days every week so often it's pretty lonely at the office (MOOC-discussion 80EC475A).*"

E. General satisfaction

In general, the respondents were very satisfied with the course and felt that their participation was worth their time and efforts. This is evidenced by the fact that of all the items of the questionnaire, the item: "Altogether it was worth participating in this course" received the most positive feedback, giving it the highest mean (M=5.63) and a median and mode of the highest possible value of 6.

Furthermore, all but two respondents indicated a likelihood of recommending the course to others with a score of 6 and above from an 11-point Likert scale. One of the two respondents was indifferent about recommending the course while the other indicated unlikelihood with a rating of four which falls on the negative end of the scale; although the least negative value. This overall positive attitude of course participants was also reflected in many of the comments posted on the MOOC platform.

Less enthusiasm was shown by participants with regards to some technical aspects of the platform. Various participants noted that the platform "*could have been easier to use*" or that it [the platform] "*was not there yet'*" technically in terms of easy navigation. In addition, users found it difficult to track their progress, which is essential in planning and managing one's time for the course. One participant gave a detailed explanation of this experience: "*It was difficult at first to find the right week and unit and coming back after a while you had to remember the name of the unit to continue. Some kind of tick-a-box-list, or any other tool for knowing how far you have studied, would have been nice."* This is clearly a current drawback of the chosen learning platform and has been reported back to the platform owners.

VI. Conclusion

International learning settings, such as those offered by MOOCs, can be beneficial for specific professional groups to engage in relevant content discussion and exchange of experiences. As confirmed by the results discussed above, professionals in the field of career guidance and employment services appreciated the content and setting of the MOOC, which supported them in their personal knowledge and skills development and even led to improved work practices, such as in the case of peer coaching.

However, the evaluation data from this MOOC have clearly shown that the engagement with peers across the globe on shared topics may not only result in knowledge gain but also contribute to the personal, affective and emotional development of the individual learners. More importantly, data have shown that constructivist online learning can strengthen the feeling of belonging to a community, especially for those professionals who may experience a feeling of isolation in terms of their geographic location or of their expertise. This particular MOOC setting was perceived as a secure space for participants to engage in trusted social interaction and peer support, similar to the group setting described by Anderson [16].

Previous studies looking on motivational aspects of participation in MOOCs found out that professionals were primarily motivated by their current needs, by which they subsumed aspect such as filling personal knowledge gaps, advancing their skillset, contributing to an increase in their work effectiveness, or enabling them to innovate. Professionals also saw the benefits of participating in MOOCs in preparing them for new roles and career progression [6].

The data obtained from this study add another motivational factor to this analysis, namely the social aspects covered in the engagement and exchange with others. When participating in cMOOCs, where emphasis is being put on the social interaction of course participants, the exchange and learning from others may also play an important motivational role for participation.

This study has only looked at feedback and comments from participants in an international MOOC, where no socio-demographic data or information about the organisational embedding of participants were collected. Further research is needed to determine what influence organisational embedding has on fulfilling learners' needs with MOOCs and whether social networks may fulfil a similar role in supporting community building and engagement for certain professions compared to a structured course with dedicated content units as offered in a MOOC environment.

TABLE I.
SUMMARY OF THE AVERAGES OF THE CLOSED ITEMS OF THE FEEDBACK QUESTIONNAIRE

Item	Topic	Statement	n	Mean	Median	Mode
1.	Content	The objectives were clear and comprehensible.	32	5.06	5.00	5.00
2.		Theoretical knowledge was provided.	32	5.22	5.00	6.00
3.		Practical knowledge and competences were provided.	32	5.16	5.00	5.00
4.		The content was communicated in a comprehensible matter.	32	5.09	5.00	6.00
5.	Participation	There was adequate room for participants' questions and interests.	32	5.38	5.50	6.00
6.	Content	The distribution of content along the time span of the course was done in an optimal way.	32	4.28	5.00	5.00
7.	Participation	There was enough attention given to reflection and experience exchange with other participants.	32	4.84	5.00	6.00
8.		My own involvement (e.g. interest, Preparation, concentrated attention, cooperation. etc.) in the course was intensive.	31	4.42	4.00	4.00
9.	Learning	I have learned something important about the Changing World of Work through this course.	30	5.17	5.00	5.00
10.		I have learned something important about peer-coaching through this course.	30	4.63	5.00	5.00
11.		I have learned something important about the digital agenda through this course.	30	5.17	5.00	5.00
12.		I have learned something important about labour market information through this course.	30	5.07	5.00	6.00
13.		I have learned something important about reflection through this course.	30	4.97	5.00	5.00
14.	Application	I can apply the learning from this course on my own professional career development.	30	5.10	5.00	6.00
15.		I am confident with using the knowledge I have gained to support the learning of others (e.g. peers, clients, employers)	30	4.93	5.00	5.00
16.	General satisfaction	Altogether it was worth participating in this course.	30	5.63	6.00	6.00
17.		How likely is it that you would recommend the course on "Changing World of Work" to others?	30	8.73	9.50	10.00
22.	Learning	The course has helped me reflect upon my own professional identity.	30	5.00	5.00	5.00

*All the items except item 17 were rated on a 7-point Likert scale of 0 to 6, whereby 0 represented "does not apply at all" and 6 "applies fully"
* Item 17 was rated on an 11-point Likert scale of 0 to 10; where 0 represented "not at all" and 10 "very likely"
* Item 18 to 21 have not been included in the table as they were open questions.

ACKNOWLEDGMENT

EmployID "Scalable & cost-effective facilitation of professional identity transformation in public employment services" is a research project supported by the ICT program of the European Commission under the 7th Framework Programme (project no. 619619).

The authors thank the whole project consortium for their input and commitment to the project.

REFERENCES

[1] J. Bimrose et al., "The Role of Facilitation in Technology-Enhanced Learning for Public Employment Services" *International Journal of Advanced Corporate Learning (iJAC)*, vol. 7, no. 3, 2014, pp. 56-65

[2] EmployID: Empowering Change in Public Employment Services. Part II, 2017

[3] A. Bandura, "Social Learning Theory," *Englewood Cliffs, NJ: Prentice Hall*, 1977.

[4] T. Bates, Comparing xMOOCs and cMOOCs: Philosophy and practice. Online Learning and Distance Education Resources. 2014. Available at: https://www.tonybates.ca/2014/10/13/comparing-xmoocs-and-cmoocs-philosophy-and-practice/ (last accessed on 1.3.2018).

[5] A. J. Gil and M. Mataveli, "Learning opportunities for group learning: An empirical assessment from the learning organization perspective," in *Journal of Workplace Learning*, vol. 29, issue: 1, 2017, pp. 65-78, https://doi.org/10.1108/JWL-02-2016-0009.

[6] C. Milligan, C., & A. Littlejohn. Why Study on a MOOC? The Motives of Students and Professionals. The International Review of Research in Open and Distributed Learning, 18(2). 2017.

[7] W. Eichhorst and A.Spermann, "Sharing Economy: Boon or Bane?" " Sharing Economy: Mehr Chancen als Risiken?," in *Wirtschaftsdienst*, vol. 96, issue 6, Springer Berlin Heidelberg, 2016, pp. 433–439.

[8] T. D. Golden, J. Veiga, and R. N. Dino, "The Impact of Professional Isolation on Teleworker Job Performance and Turnover Intentions: Does Time Spent Teleworking, Interacting Face-to-Face, or Having Access to Communication-Enhancing Technology Matter?" in the *Journal of applied psychology*, vol. 93, 2008, pp. 1412–1421.

[9] M. A. Orhan, J. B. Rijsman, and G. M. Van Dijk, "Invisible, therefore isolated: Comparative effects of team virtuality with task virtuality on workplace isolation and work outcomes," in *Revista de Psicología del Trabajo y de las Organizaciones*, vol. 2, issue: 2, 2016, pp.109–122.

[10] G. Attwell et. al, *EmployID: Empowering Change in Public Employment Services. Part II*, 2017

[11] W. R. Shadish, D. T Cook, and D.T. Campbell, *Experimental and Quasi-Experimental Designs for Generalized Causal Inference*, Belmont, CA: Wadsworth Cengage Learning, 2002.

[12] M. L. Mitchell and J. M. Jolley, *Research Design Explained*, 7th Edition, Belmont, CA: Wadsworth Cengage Learning, 2010.

[13] B. H. Erickson and T. A. Nosanchuk, *Understanding data (second edition)*, Berkshire, England, Open University Press, 2009.

[14] H. Hsieh and S. E. Shannon, "Three Approaches to Qualitative Content Analysis," *Qualitative Health Research*, Vol. 15, issue 9, pp. 1277-1288, November 2005.

[15] P. Mayring, "Qualitative Content Analysis", *Forum: Qualitative Social Research*, Vol. 1.2, Art. 20, June 2000.

[16] T. Anderson, "*Theories for learning with emerging technologies,* In G. Veletsianos (Ed.), Emergence and Innovation in Digital **Learning**: Foundations and Applications (pp. 35-50). Edmonton: Athabasca University Press. 2016.

AUTHORS

Barbara Kieslinger is with the Department of Technology and Knowledge, Centre for Social Innovation, Vienna, Austria (e-mail: kieslinger@zsi.at).

Juliet Tschank is with the Department of Work and Equal Opportunities, Centre for Social Innovation, Vienna, Austria (e-mail: tschank@zsi.at)

Teresa Schäfer, is with the Department of Technology and Knowledge, Centre for Social Innovation, Vienna, Austria (e-mail: schaefer@zsi.at).

Claudia Magdalena Fabian, is with the Department of Technology and Knowledge, Centre for Social Innovation, Vienna, Austria (e-mail: fabian@zsi.at).

Manuscript received 28 March 2018. This work was supported in part by the European Union under Grant FP7 – 619619.

Published as submitted by the author(s).

Teaching Technology Usage in the ENT Medical Subdomain via a Flipped Classroom Approach

Walter Koch[1], Jochen Schachenreiter[2], Klaus Vogt[3], Gerda Koch[4] and Wolfgang Göderle[5]

[1] Steinbeis Transfer Center for Information Management, Medical and Cultural Heritage Informatics, Graz, Austria

[2] Medical Practice Schachenreiter, Graz, Austria

[3] University of Latvia, Riga/Center of Experimental Medicine, Latvia

[4] AIT Angewandte Informationstechnik Forschungsgesellschaft mbH, Graz, Austria

[5] Karl-Franzens-University/History Department, Graz, Austria

***Abstract*—The flipped classroom approach is supporting a continuous interaction of students and instructors via online communication and strengthens the ability to solve problems by self-organization. This is especially important in medical domains, like the one of ENT-Head/Neck (ENT: Ear-Nose-Throat) surgeries and treatment. Surgical corrections of the nasal airways, like FESS (Functional Endoscopy Sinus Surgery) or in the field of plastic surgery, are the second frequent surgical interventions in otorhinolaryngology. They have to be prepared very carefully and airflow simulation with Computational Fluid Dynamics (CFD) is gaining importance for diagnostics here. New in silico procedures, like imaging, 3D modelling, CFD simulation and analysis, are to be part of a standard clinical pathway in the ENT domain in the near future. The project Rhinodiagnost.eu for instance will extend the morphological diagnostics by detailed functional analysis, i.e. the visualization of the nasal air stream and the physical analysis of its energetic. In order to train ENT specialists on the new diagnostic aids Rhinodiagnost.eu will provide flipped classroom online lessons using the tool "Mediathread" of the Columbia University, as learning environment.**

***Index Terms*—Flipped Classroom, Ear-Nose-Throat Treatment, CFD simulation, 3D modelling.**

I. Introduction

"Flipped classroom", a type of blended learning, is a preferred method for knowledge transfer to students and among all kind of members within institutions. Using this method the instructor adopts the role of a coach and encourages the learners to interact and to contribute content themselves. This method strengthens the ability to solve problems by self-organization [1] which is especially important in medical domains, like the one of ENT-Head/Neck (ENT: Ear-Nose-Throat) surgeries and treatment. In this medical field new in silico procedures, like imaging, 3D modelling, CFD (Computational Fluid Dynamics) simulation and analysis, are to be part of a standard clinical pathway in the ENT domain in the near future. Surgical corrections of the nasal airways, like FESS (Functional Endoscopy Sinus Surgery) or in the field of plastic surgery, are the second frequent surgical interventions in otorhinolaryngology. They have to be prepared very carefully and airflow simulation via CFD is gaining importance for diagnostics here. The project Rhinodiagnost.eu for instance will extend the morphological diagnostics by detailed functional analysis, i.e. the visualization of the nasal airflow and the physical analysis of its energetic. The visualization and simulation of airflows from the nostrils to the nasal pharynx afford a precise and high quality 3D reconstruction of the nasal cavities. And the successive validation and interpretation of CFD simulation results is a challenge for non CFD specialists. Therefore Rhinodiagnost.eu project will use the flipped classroom online tool *Mediathread,* developed by the Columbia University, as learning environment. With *Mediathread* "compositions" for explaining specific concepts like: image processing, 3D modelling, CFD simulations, definition and processing of clinical pathways, are published and "assignments" to students, asking to elaborate on various topics may be issued. The continuous interaction of students and instructors via *Mediathread* will support medical technical competence development according to the knowledge maturity model.

A. New Learning Technologies

With the introduction of online courses and networked information services higher education and workplace learning has changed tremendously. Digital technologies have gained huge influence on how we learn and how we obtain information. A new emphasis is put on the benefits of active (online) learner's participation. Collective content development and learning in networked communities is seen as a means to filter out the right content for our needs from the mass of information provided globally. Open (online) communication with team members and learning partners creates synergies and new insights into issues making it easier to create innovative solutions, creative alternatives, and new goals.

In modern learning environments, the learners move to the centre and the choice of learning resources is closely related to the professional context. Within virtual learning platforms joint knowledge bases are built and the participatory contributions of learners and trainers can be clearly arranged and stored and additionally be kept ready for repeated training. This makes it easier to later build upon existing content, in order to expand the wealth of experience, the knowledge base. Preparing Micro learning compositions, which implies packing the learning content into small lessons, provides the advantage of rapid adaptability and structuring of the knowledge. That way, the learner can consume the content quickly and flexibly [2].

Studies have shown that up to 80% of activity-based knowledge is acquired through informal learning, such as questioning, observing or trying out [3]. Collaborative learning environments support this form of competence building as the focus shifts from the teacher to the learner and knowledge is generated collectively through interaction and the learning of teams [4].

II. New Technologies For the ENT Medical Subdomain

A. *Additional Diagnostic Tools for ENT Diagnostics*

About 11% of the European population suffers from an obstruction of nasal breathing or an inflammation of the nasal sinuses [5]. For patients affected the quality of life can be severely limited. In Germany, Austria and Switzerland, more than 100,000 surgeries on the nose or the nasal sinuses are carried out annually. In the US, more than 500,000 nasal and sino-nasal surgeries per year are performed [6]. But the present diagnosis of nasal function is not accurate enough, in order to provide always a clearly verifiable indication for nasal surgeries.

Computational Fluid Dynamics (CFD) as a methodology to visualize the airflow in nasal and paranasal sinuses has been topic of many scientific papers during the last decades. To know and see whether airflow enters a paranasal sinus or not is important for the ENT surgeon preparing a surgery in a paranasal sinus. But integrating CFD-Simulation into a day to day clinical operation is still an open issue due to the complexity and multidisciplinarity of this approach. The involvement of highly experienced medical experts, fluid dynamic experts, as well as informatics experts – only to name a few – in combination with expensive computer hardware (HPC High Performance Computing) has made it nearly impossible in the past to make CFD-simulations available for the established ENT-specialist.

Current research projects try to change this situation and put a focus on the validation of CFD results and on the integration of different methodologies (3D models, CFD simulations) into a virtual surgery device for preparing ENT surgeries. They also aim to include 3D visualization and CFD simulation into the standard clinical pathway for ENT treatment. In September 2017 the European Union-funded project Rhinodiagnost (www.rhinodiagnost.eu) started. The project will establish coordinated morphological and functional diagnostics services for ENT physicians [7]. New, additional decision aids, such as 3D models and flow simulations, shall be offered to ENT physicians and radiologists. Project partners within Rhinodiagnost.eu are renowned research centers like the Technical University of Aachen, the Supercomputing Center Juelich, and several privately owned companies in the information and medical-technical sector. Rhinodiagnost.eu will provide a network of easy accessible and low-cost service points for these diagnostic services and targets to introduce these technologies as standard means for ENT diagnostics. The supplied information surplus will allow surgeons and practitioners that are trained on the new technologies to improve patient-individual operation and treatment planning. In the long run the use of the services should raise the success rate of surgeries and of treatments.

III. Teaching Technology Usage for ENT Specialists

A. *Implementing a Flipped Classroom Approach*

Training for highly qualified occupations needs to focus to a great extent on strengthening the ability to solve problems by self-organization and enabling the learner to recognize connections between subjects, ideas and concepts. Competence development is basically fostered by the assessment of observable behavior and action [8]. Collaborative online learning environments that put the focus on the learner and the knowledge creation through the interactive learning of teams support these training principles [9]. In a flipped classroom environment the teacher adopts the role of a trainer or coach [10] and the self-organized interaction between the learners or trainees is the central source of knowledge transfer. Knowledge is mostly assembled via social exchange, the guidance of a tutor and the delivery of self-created content. Therefore, an online platform for flipped classroom learning should support the creation of structured micro learning units, the integration of a wide variety of multimedia content (video, audio, images, texts etc.), the collection and management of external resources, the assignment of tasks, and should include easy-to-use functionalities for online cooperation, communication, discussion and feedback.

The Rhinodiagnost.eu project looked for a tool that would not just offer a comprehensive learning management or content management system, but rather support the participatory design and documentation of subject areas. Evaluation of various platforms resulted in the adoption of the open source platform *Mediathread* (http://mediathread.columbia.edu/) for Rhinodiagnost.eu purposes. *Mediathread* has been developed by the Columbia Center for New Media Teaching and Learning at Columbia University since 2010 and is used in a variety of courses, including at other American universities. The focus of *Mediathread* is on providing a platform for the preparation, management and analysis of online multimedia content. The tool works very well with a small, focused scholarly community or seminar, supporting connections, open access, and networked learning. The platform enables the linking and integration of content from various external media platforms such as *YouTube*, *Flickr*, the *Internet Archive*, *Vimeo*, *Wikimedia Commons*, *Pinterest* or *Kaltura*. Using *Mediathread* the content can be further edited, annotated, organized and embedded in texts. It is possible to link descriptions to external content and enrich them. Instructors and coaches can coordinate respective threads. The tool also supports the creation of short assignments or questions that learners and team members need to work on and contribute online. Thus, step by step, a knowledge base is built cooperatively.

Mediathread does not upload multimedia data (videos, pictures, audios) to the system, but simply refers to the content and embeds it in the courses of the platform. Doing this a student can contribute information of his or her own interest into a lesson. There, the content can be further distributed, annotated, tailored and referenced in the discussion and knowledge contributions. In addition, it is also possible for administrators or tutors to enable an upload function for existing local multimedia content.

For the ENT case the tool *Mediathread* provides the possibility of elaborating "compositions" which can either explain a specific concept like: image processing, 3D modelling, CFD simulations, definition and processing of clinical pathways, etc. or present an "assignment" to a student, asking to elaborate on various topics. Through the continuous interaction of students and instructors the *Mediathread* platform is enhanced in an iterative process.

B. *ENT Training with Mediathread*

Research in Rhiodiagnost.eu and other related projects [11] has brought forward that a comprehensive diagnostic tool-kit for ENT practitioners and radiologists ought to include visualization of the nasal cavities (using 3D modelling), the execution of CFD-simulation, and in special cases even the print out of 3D models of pathological regions of interest. The 3D mesh generated from the CT DICOM-images allows the doctors and surgeons to view the diseased areas from all perspectives, making it possible to virtually zoom into the tiniest regions and holes. Hence, the mesh of the paranasal sinuses is an important aid for the planning and preparation of e.g. Functional Endoscopic Sinus Surgery (FESS) and can be used for education and training on FESS. When conducting a Functional Endoscopic Sinus Surgery an endoscope, a thin fibre-optic tube, is used to improve ventilation and drainage and to remove polyps. With the endoscope and specialized tools the surgeon removes unusual and obstructive tissues through the nostrils. This technique has now been used for several decades in treating sino-nasal conditions and the extent of each surgery depends on the severity of the disease and the surgeon's individual practice.

Figure 1. Preparation of a composition on FESS

Fig. 1 shows the composition panel. Left the information texts are entered which are enriched with media items selected from the media "Collection" list on the right hand side. Media used to enrich the written information may be annotated and in extracts selected for the course.

For making the adequate diagnosis of Chronic rhinosinusitis (CRS) a check-up is carried out by the ENT-Head/Neck surgery specialist. In addition to the anamnesis, a nose endoscopy and a spiral Computed Tomography (CT) of the paranasal sinuses is done, which should preferably be carried out in an inflammation-free interval. The extent of shading of the paranasal sinuses in the CT and the anatomical relationships determine the severity of CRS [16]. However, the 2-dimensional images of the conventional CT examination of the paranasal sinuses merely give an idea of the ventilation of the sinuses. But current developments in the field of numerical flow mechanics and high-performance calculations are permitting patient-individual computer-assisted flow predictions that can help to detect and limit the anatomical location of pathologies. A CFD simulation of the nose and the paranasal sinuses can be performed [12], [13]. With this method, the inner nose can be virtually traversed, and the slight flows in the area of the paranasal sinuses, especially the very narrow passages, can be visualized [14], [15]. The main advantage for the radiologist and the ENT-Head-neck surgeon is that additionally to the static CT-examination the CFD will show the dynamic function of the ventilation in the nasal cavity and the paranasal sinuses. This improves both: sensitivity and specificity in the assessment of pathologies like eg. a Chronic rhinosinusitis (CRS).

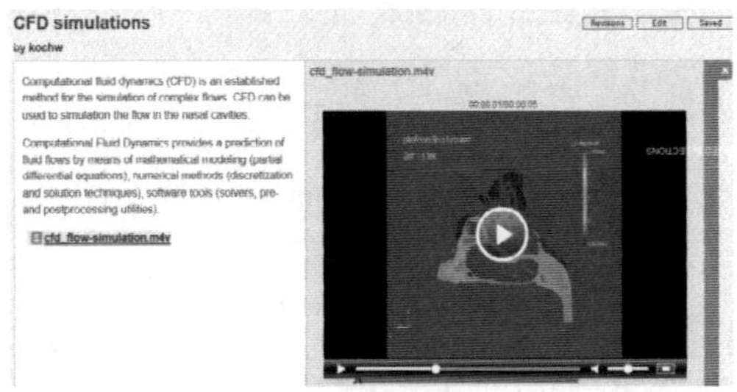

Figure 2. Preparation of a composition on FESS

Fig. 2 shows part of a composition on the basic principles of CFD attached with a video on the simulation of a nasal airflow.

In order to correctly use and interpret the results of the 3D meshes and the CFD simulation doctors and surgeons need to be trained on these new technologies. Surgeons shall be able to use both technologies to improve surgery planning and to simulate possible post-surgery scenarios. For that it is important to know what the CFD simulation tells about the airflow, and how to use and interpret the 3D mesh generated out of the DICOM images. Fig. 3 shows the micro learning unit on 3D meshes where a short introduction on image-based meshing from computed tomography data for medical specialists is provided.

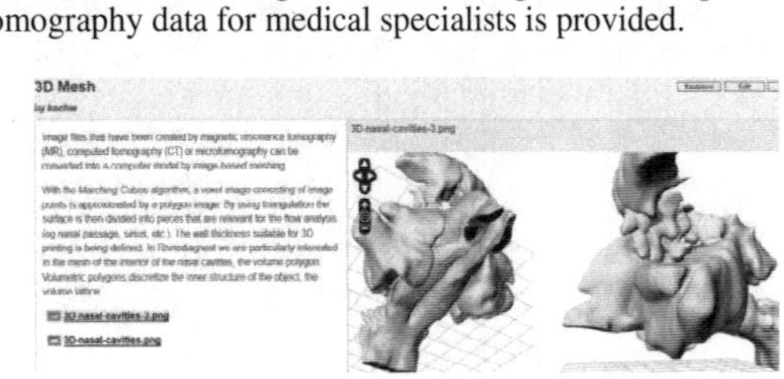

Figure 3. Composition on 3D meshing

CFD and 3D meshes render diagnostics more precisely and both technologies can also be applied in training, for virtual surgery or for producing 3D printed training models for surgeons-to-be. 3D printing provides important additional information for difficult surgeries in selected regions of interest [17]. Fig. 4 depicts parts of a composition on this topic.

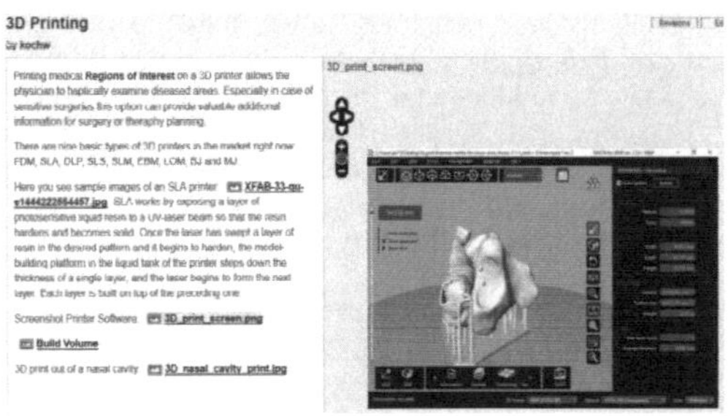

Figure 4. Introduction to 3D printing

500.000 FESS-surgeries are taking place every year in the US only, an amount of about 2.000 surgeries per working day or 300 per working hour is a reasonable figure [18], [19], [20]. Therefore, it is important to optimize the different activities in the surgery preparation workflow. Standard clinical pathways reduce variations in practice and align decisions with evidence-based medicine, operational efficiency, and quality. The Object Management Group (http://www.omg.org/), being an international, open membership, not-for-profit technology standards consortium, has started in 2016 an initiative, the "Health BPM Pilot", to standardize the description of clinical procedures. In October 2017 a draft version of the "Field Guide to Shareable Clinical Pathways" was issued. The Health BPM Pilot strongly advocates the use of standards like the Business Process Modelling and Notation (BPMN), the Decision Management and Notation (DMN), or the Case Management Model and Notation (CMMN) for the design process of clinical pathways. It is important that ENT specialists are able to read business process models conceptualized with standard notations in order to contribute to the clinical pathway discussion. Fig. 5 shows a *Mediathread* discussion based on an assignment on standard modelling notations.

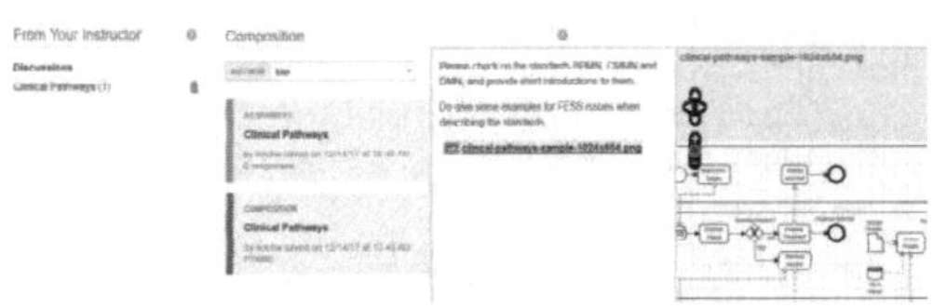

Figure 5. Assigning and discussing the use of standard notations

The first draft version of the *Mediathread* training course created by Rhinodiagnost.eu focuses on basic knowledge transfer for Computational Fluid Dynamics, 3D meshing and 3D printing for ENT specialists. Medical practitioners and students should get a basic understanding of these technologies and how they can be used in ENT diagnostics. As new technologies are further intruding into all work areas the course will be constantly adapted and enhanced. Finally, the course platform should provide a growing source of knowledge for ENT experts and a means for international discussion and sharing of experiences with the new diagnostic tools. Currently, a new composition on machine learning and convolutional neural networks is being set up. Since the radio source of the CT is operated with the weakest possible intensity, for the benefit of the patient, not all structures in the CT images are optimally recorded. Therefore the images need to be re-worked in order to serve as proper basis for the 3D visualization and mesh generation. This happens either via a time-consuming manual post processing processes or with the help of machine learning and convolutional neural networks (CNN) [21, 22]. The CNN can be trained to detect automatically whether a point of the CT scan (DICOM image) is located inside or outside of a nasal (or paranasal) sinus. This will lead in the long run not only to quick image segmentation and 3D processing but also to a classification indicating the pathological condition of a nasal or paranasal sinus.

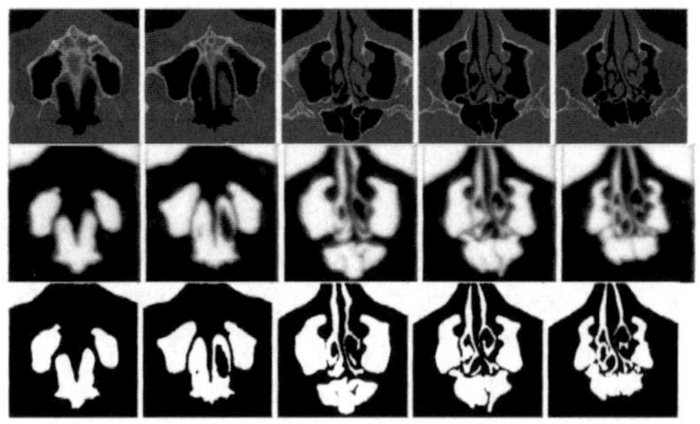

Figure 6. CT images and CNN supported segmentation

IV. Conclusion

Novel diagnostic tools using CFD simulation and 3D visualization will be provided to ENT specialists and radiologists in the near future. These tools can be offered via rapid networks to ENT practitioners and radiologists. But students and doctors need to be trained to work with the new tools and to correctly assess their diagnostic input. The Rhinodiganost.eu project uses the *Mediathread* platform as a flipped classroom environment to offer training for the Rhinodiagnost morphological and functional ENT diagnostic services. The courses teach students and doctors how to use CFD simulations, 3D meshing or 3D printing, and introduce into topics like business process modelling for clinical pathways or machine learning. All courses offer introductory online compositions, assignments for participants, media material and the possibility to interact with a tutor or coach. Trainees may actively shape and contribute online to a joint knowledge base thus strengthening their ability of self-organization, networked collaboration and digital competence.

References

[1] G. Siemens, "Connectivism: A Learning Theory for the Digital Age," in *International Journal of Instructional Technology and Distance Learning*, vol. 2, no. 1, pp. 3–10, 2005.

[2] G. Siemens, "Connectivism: Creating a Learning Ecology in Distributed Environments," in: *Didactics of microlearning.*

Concepts, discourses and examples, Hug, Theo (Eds.), 2007, pp. 53–68.

[3] G. Attwell, "Personal Learning Environments - the future of eLearning?," in *eLearning Papers*, vol. 2, no. 1, 2007.

[4] P. M. Senge, "*The Fifth Discipline: The Art & Practice of The Learning Organization*." Crown Publishing Group, 2010.

[5] D. Hastan, et al., "Chronic Rhinosinusitis in Europe – an underestimated disease. A GA^{2}LEN study", in *Allergy*, vol 66, no. 9, 2011. doi:10.1111/j.1398-9995.2011.02646.x.

[6] N. Bhattacharyya, "Ambulatory sinus and nasal surgery in the United States: demographics and perioperative outcomes", in *Laryngoscope*, vol. 120, no. 3, pp. 635-8, 2010. doi: 10.1002/lary.20777.

[7] A. Lintermann, J.H. Göbbert, K. Vogt, W. Koch, and A. Hetzel, "Rhinodiagnost - Morphological and functional precision diagnostics of nasal cavities", in *InSiDE, Innovatives Supercomputing in Deutschland*, vol. 15, no. 2, pp. 106-109, 2017.

[8] A. Bolder, "Arbeit, Qualifikation und Kompetenzen," in *Handbuch Bildungsforschung. 2. Ed.*, Tippelt, Rudolf/Schmidt, Bernhard, Hrsg., 2009, pp. 813–843.

[9] H. Lee, C. J. Bonk, "Collaborative Learning in the Workplace. Practical Issues and Concerns," in *International Journal of Advanced Corporate Learning (iJAC)*, vol. 7, no. 2, p. 10, 2014. DOI: 10.3991/ijac.v7i2.3850.

[10] F. Böhm, „*Der Tele-Tutor. Betreuung Lehrender und Lernender im virtuellen Raum*," VS Verlag für Sozialwissenschaften, GWV Fachverlage GmbH Wiesbaden, 2006.

[11] J. Schachenreiter, G. Ranner, W. Koch, R. Jakse, and M. Wu, „Verification of the Ventilation of the Paranasal Sinuses using Computational Fluid Dynamics (CFD)," unpublished.

[12] S. K. Kim, Y. Na, J.-I. Kim, and S.-K. Chung, "Patient specific CFD models of nasal airflow: Overview of methods and challenges," in *Journal of Biomechanics*, Special Issue: Biofluid Mechanics, vol. 46, no. 2, Jan. 2013, pp. 299–306.

[13] D. J. Doorly, D. J. Taylor, A. M. Gambaruto, R. C. Schroter, and N. Tolley, "Nasal Architecture: Form and Flow," in *Philosophical Transactions of the Royal Society of London A: Mathematical, Physical and Engineering Sciences*, vol. 366, no. 1879, Sep. 2008, pp. 3225–46.

[14] S. Zachow, A. Steinmann, T. Hildebrandt, R. Weber, and W. Heppt, "CFD simulation of nasal airflow: towards treatment planning for functional rhinosurgery," in *International Journal of Computer Assisted Radiology and Surgery*, Jun. 2006, pp. 165-167.

[15] R. Mösges, B. Büchner, M. Kleiner, R. Freitas, I. Hörschler, and W. Schröder, "Computational fluid dynamics analysis of nasal flow," in *B-ENT*, vol. 6, no. 3, Jan. 2010, pp. 161–165.

[16] W. J. Fokkens, V. J. Lund, J. Mullol, C. Bachert, I. Alobid, F. Baroody et al., "European Position Paper on Rhinosinusitis and Nasal Polyps 2012," in *Rhinology*, vol. 50, sup. 23, Mar. 2012, pp. 201-207.

[17] K.K. VanKoevering, K.M. Malloy, "Emerging Role of Three-Dimensional Printing in Simulation in Otolaryngology," in Simulation in Otolaryngology, Otolaryngologic Clinics of North Amerika, vol. 50, no. 5, Oct. 2017, pp. 98-110.

[18] K. A. Smith, R. R. Orlandi, and L. Rudmik. "Cost of adult chronic rhinosinusitis: a systematic review," in *The Laryngoscope*, vol. 125, no. 7, Jan. 2015, pp. 1547–1556.

[19] W. Fokkens, V. Lund, C. Bachert, P. Clement, P. Helllings, M. Holmstrom et al., "EAACI Position Paper on Rhinosinusitis and Nasal Polyps Executive Summary," in *Allergy*, vol. 60, no. 5, May 2005, pp. 583–601.

[20] M. A. Pynnonen, and M. M. Davis, "Extent of sinus surgery, 2000 to 2009: A population-based study," in *The Laryngoscope*, vol. 124, no. 4, Apr. 2014, pp. 820–825.

[21] S. Wang, and R. M. Summers, "Machine Learning and Radiology," in *Medical Image Analysis*, vol. 16, no. 5, Jul. 2012, pp. 933–51.

[22] J.-G. Lee, S. Jun, Y.-W. Cho, H. Lee, G. Bae Kim, J. Beom Seo, and N. Kim, "Deep Learning in Medical Imaging: General Overview," in *Korean Journal of Radiology*, vol. 18, no. 4, Aug. 2017, pp. 570–84.

AUTHORS

Univ.Prof.Dr. Walter Koch, is with Steinbeis Transfer Center for Information Management, Medical and Cultural Heritage Informatics, Klosterwiesgasse 32/1, A-8010 Graz, Austria (e-mail: walter.koch@stw.de).

Dr.med. Jochen Schachenreiter, is with Medical Practice Schachenreiter, Elisabethstrasse 81, A-8010 Graz, Austria (e-mail: ordination@schachenreiter.at).

Univ.Prof.Dr. Klaus Vogt, MD, DDS, is with University of Latvia, Center of Experimental Medicine, Raiņa bulvāris 19, Centra rajons, Rīga, LV-1586, Lettland (e-mail: rhinovogt@t-online.de).

Mag. Gerda Koch MBA, is with AIT Angewandte Informationstechnik Forschungsgesellschaft mbH, Klosterwiesgasse 32/1, A-8010 Graz, Austria (e-mail: kochg@ait.co.at).

Mag.Dr. Wolfgang Göderle, is with Karl Franzens-University Graz, Attemsgasse 8/IV, A-8010 Graz, Austria (e-mail: wolfgang.goederle@uni-graz.at).

Manuscript received 15 March 2018. This work is supported in part by the EU-Programme COIN/IraSME under Grant 861510.

Published as submitted by the author(s).

Distance Learning in the Musical Field in Romania through European-Funded Projects

Nelida Nedelcuţ[1], Gabriel Ciprian Pop[1] and Amalia Cristina Nedelcuţ[2]

[1] Academy of Music Gheorghe Dima/Department of Distance Education, Cluj-Napoca, Romania

[2]Babes-Bolyai University, Faculty of Economics and Business Administration/Management Department, Cluj-Napoca, Romania

***Abstract*—The organization of Romanian distance learning in music has been supported in terms of research, collaboration and financing by European projects, with the following achievements: training of teaching staff involved in distance learning, assistance in activities meant to introduce ICT in general schools, construction of a platform dedicated to distance learning activities, creating a database with instrumental accompaniments for singers, designing multimedia courses, assessing distance learning programs offered by the Academy of Music Gheorghe Dima in Cluj-Napoca.**

The Prelude Training Programme on ICT in Music Education – a project aimed at developing a training programme for in-service music educators, as there are many ways in which technology helps educators meet instructional goals: Programs designed to help students develop their musicianship or improve their knowledge of notation and skill in reading notation, support with improvisation skills, notation and sequencing programs which assist students in composition activities.

Vemus - Virtual European Music Schools - a programme which focuses on teaching music notation or performing instruments, involving execution of rhythm patterns, melody, music scores; E-vocal learning, with simultaneous appearance of sound and notation, conducted by famous musicians. DIMA - Direct Impact of Multimedia Application - a platform that comprises courses, audio and video examples focusing on music history, performing and listening activities.

The partners proceed from various areas (higher education, innovation/development centers), and the projects were conceived to stimulate the implementation of ICT in the educational process in music, approaching teaching staff as a target group, and students as an interested party.

The need for such products was revealed by interviews and questionnaires and the results' evaluation proved that the online environment can be accessed in order to develop educational resources, enrich lesson content, motivate and engage children in music education, deliver information and learning opportunities, stimulate children in their musical endeavors.

***Index Terms*—EU project, educational platform, training teachers, music, Romanian dissemination, IT magazine, multimedia applications, national grants.**

I. Introduction

The introduction of information and communication technology in music has created interdisciplinary fields that have subsequently established a basis for various disciplines such as: musicology, computer-assisted composition, acoustics, sound processing, psychoacoustics, interfering to an equal extent with principles from physics, electronics, informatics, and social sciences. In current electronic music, as the virtualization of the work environment increases with every day that goes by, the tools most frequently used are computer software and software suites which offer media for recording, synthesis, manipulation, arrangement of the audio material beside the usual hardware found in studios. One of the most important advantages of using the virtual environment is the fact that, on the whole, everything is cheaper and much more versatile (1). The market is literally flooded with a range of software and software suites that can be used to create music, the number and the features of which can be confusing. Nevertheless, a careful analysis of all these tools can reveal a series of mutual elements which, once assimilated, can establish a starting point in learning how to use them (2).

Music education through the use of ICT posed a challenge for all institutions due to the complexity of the methods and processes involved in the system, and the solutions offered in various European countries were the result of research and experiments validated by notable outcomes [3], [4], [5], [6]. Various perspectives in the use of information and communication technology triggered the development of learning methods such as creative and collaborative learning, which have had a very dynamic evolution, each year bringing about innovations and improvements. The directions pursued by the endeavors of experts in the field of music focused on the impact of ICT in music education, designing specialized software [7] as well as educational platforms targeted at a range of users from novice students to professional musicians [8]. The topic of distance learning has become a highly current issue and has been developed in European projects which finance new methods and techniques specific to the field of music and study the impact of distance learning in education. A higher number of complete courses and entire degree programs in music education have thus become accessible [9]. In order to motivate people to introduce ICT in music education, it is recommended to access the online environment for the accomplishment of the following purposes:

- Development of educational resources;
- Enrichment of lesson content by accessing information on-line;
- Motivation and engagement of children in music education;
- Provision of information and learning opportunities in ways that are attractive to children;
- Stimulation of children to perform their own musical investigations [10].

In Romania, the challenges faced in introducing this type of education were linked to insufficient knowledge of using ICT materials by educators, on the one hand, and, on the other hand, to the inexistence of data bases that would have facilitated the planning of a building process for an IT-based educational system in music. The introduction of distance learning in the field of music in Romania benefited by the experience of prestigious European institutions; the need for a rapid implementation of the educational methods specific to this type of education determined the Academy of Music Gheorghe Dima (AMGD), as an institution accredited for the provision of undergraduate programs in the form of distance learning, to approach effective teaching/learning techniques. The high number of unqualified teaching staff who were providing teaching or artistic activities in various institutions motivated AMGD to organize music education programs by distance learning and, to this end, to have its own staff trained in the use of information technology and to create workplaces in order to receive an education.

The undergraduate programs have attracted numerous people in search of a qualification, leading to a continuous request for distance learning education over the past ten years.

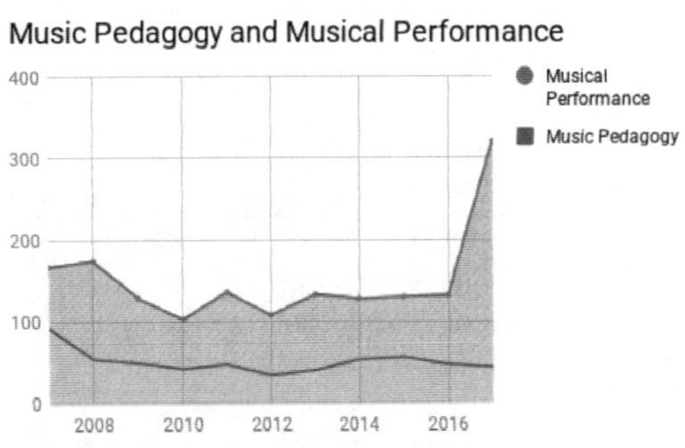

Figure 1. The dynamics of students enrolled in distance learning programs in AMGD

In the construction stages of the undergraduate programs the teaching staff attended numerous training courses meant to teach them how to create learning materials. The infrastructure necessary for the development of distance learning programs in AMGD was provided by means of a research project financed by the World Bank. The access to European research networks in the field of ICT in music enabled participants to get acquainted with the features of the e-learning system and the opportunities of adapting it to the musical field. Between 2006 and 2014 the institution received European funding as partner or subcontractor, in projects that made a considerable contribution to the construction of distance learning in the musical field in Romania, such as:

TABEL I
EUROPEAN PROJECTS

PROJECT	Financing line/subject	Partners
Prelude - Training Programme on ICT in Music Education SOCRATES COMENIUS 2.1 Action (Training of School Education Staff)	A training EU Programme on ICT in Music Education higher education, innovation/ development centre	Ellinigermaniki Agogi (GR), Roehampton University (UK), Enterprise Walding (AT), Sonic Interactive Institute (SE), Centre of Innovation, Academy of Music Gh. Dima (RO), Institution Sek Ciudalcampo (ES), Miksike (EE).
Vemus -Virtual European Music Schools Framework Programme 6 (Technologies for the Information Society – IST).	Virtual instruments, psychoacoustics, Artificial Intelligence, and Human-Computer Interaction.	Institute for Language and Speech Processing (GR), Centre National de Creation Musicale (FR), Royal Institute of Technology (SE), Ellinigermaniki Agogi (GR), Balteck (LT), Philippos Nakas S.A. (GR), Miksike Learning Folders Ltd. (EE), Centrul pentru Dezvoltare și Inovare în Educație (RO).
E-vocal learning Lifelong Learning, Programme Creativity and Innovation	Design of an e-learning platform for singing on the web	Vokalakademie (AT), Concorde International (U), Fachhochschule Wedel (DE), Rózsavölgyi Márk Müvészeti Iskola (HU), VHS Poly College, Wiener Volksbühne (AT)
Dima -Direct Impact of Multimedia Application-Exploratory research project PN II Idei	Exploration of the adaptation of on-line educational materials to music teaching;	Academy of Music Gheorghe Dima (RO).

II. PRELUDE PROJECT OVERWIEW

Prelude was an EU project that provided mainly a training programme for in-service music teachers. The main target was to stimulate the implementation of IT in the teaching/learning process in the music education area. The project milestones:

- The preliminary survey consisted in: interviews held with the selected teachers and questionnaires addressed to music teachers of the consortium, then drafting a synoptic table concerning the music education system in the partners' countries;

- The Prelude training programme with conventional courses and workshops;

- The creation of the Prelude distance learning platform

The initial inquiry, organized in order to identify "The teachers' needs" highlighted various shortcomings and training needs in the participant countries. The conclusion was that each partner of the consortium must organize teacher training according to their own training plan. In AMGD, we applied the following evaluation tools:

a) interviews held with the selected teachers (teachers of theory and musical instruments)

b) two questionnaires applied to 25 teachers; the first questionnaire comprised 12 questions focusing on the evaluation of ICT degrees, and the second had 10 questions aiming at identifying the evolution trend of IT in the following five years. This highlighted necessities linked to the following shortcomings:

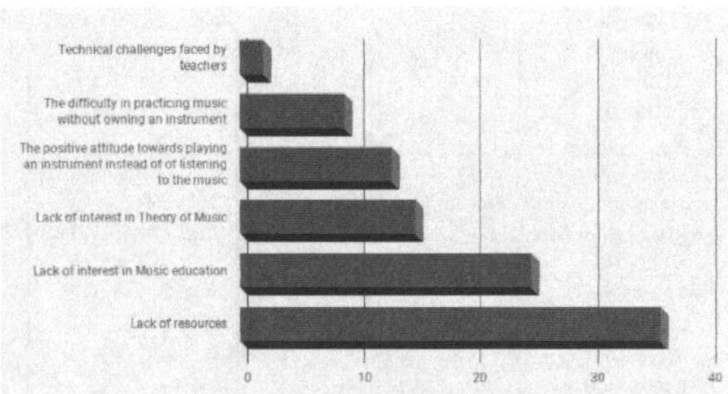

Figure 2. The problems encountered in the educational process

The main result of the project was connected with the opportunity to train teaching staff from each participant institution based on a training programme for in-service music teachers created by the experienced institutions in the project, in which technology sought to address the instructional goals of music teachers in each particular country. These include: programs designed to help students develop their musicianship or improve their knowledge of notation and skill in reading notation or improvisation skills, simultaneous appearance of sound and notation, programs which focus on teaching music notation or performing aural tests involving recognition and dictation of rhythm patterns, melody patterns, musical intervals, chord sequences and harmonic progressions, notation and sequencing programs which assist students in composing activities.

An electronic platform based on *Moodle* was launched, with the following facilities:

- Search the list of courses
- Have access to materials in various formats (text, video, audio, link on the web)
- Edit or update profiles
- Download teacher assignments
- Reflect on proposed materials and upload feedback
- Use the communication facilities
- Present students' own questions and answers
- Get informed about events, news or class activities
- Participate in the assessment

The PRELUDE project represents a paradigm of the distance education plan that seeks to employ the advantages of Open and Distance Learning (ODL) instruments and techniques in order to provide:

- Quality in service training to music teachers
- Professional support to trainees
- Testing and reflective feedback on suggested teaching activities
- Formation of groups and communities amongst the participants

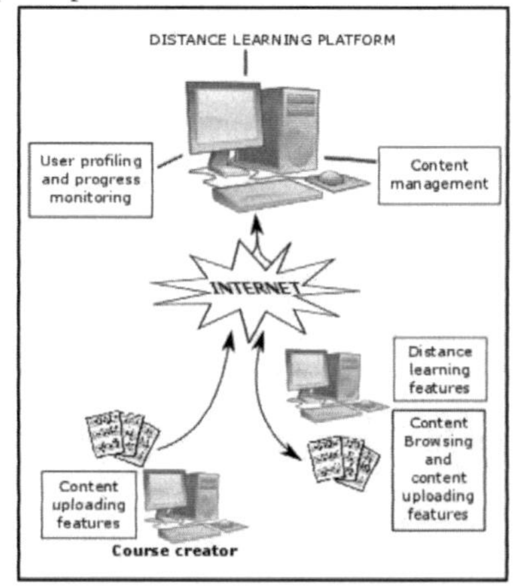

Figure 3. Prelude Platform chart

Prelude Platform was based on the Moodle (acronym for Modular Object-Oriented Dynamic Learning Environment) free educational software package – an excellent open source and free Learning Management System. Moodle was chosen because of its functionalities that include: Multi-lingual choice, not specific hardware requirements, respect for international learning standards, personalization for the learner, easy installing and managing, detailed monitoring for students, tools for content creation, assessment for the students, various forms of communication, etc. – all with the advantage of free software status.

TABLE II
PRELUDE PROJECT OUTPUTS

Project products	Accomplishments of AMGD
a) a platform (web page for personal projects, links connected to similar sites and libraries online), and a bulletin/newsletter (PRELUDE training platform); b) a guide of good practice issued in electronic and classic format, disseminated among all interested people; c) editing a CD containing this guide, as well as the latest edition of the project's web page (PRELUDE CD-ROM).	access to experience in the music field in European countries; training of Romanian teaching staff in using electronic platforms and ICT in music classes; specialization of the tutors and coordinators involved in the distance learning activities in AMGD; assistance from specialists in activities linked to the introduction of ICT in general schools; construction of an interactive platform dedicated to distance activities

After organizing training workshops for teachers in several schools in Romania, they showed interest in becoming acquainted with and using ICT in music classes. The access to the Prelude information base also led to the specialization of coordinators and tutors from AMGD, who subsequently contributed to building the distance learning system in the institution.

After finalizing the project, the training of teaching staff in the use of ICT in the musical field continued, as AMGD organized training programs meant to integrate ICT on two levels:

- training courses for the tutors and coordinators in the institutions (2/year)

- research projects in IT, for example exploration of the adaptation of on-line educational tools to the artistic-musical education, a project financed by the Ministry of Research in Romania.

III. VIRTUAL EUROPEAN MUSIC SCHOOL

VEMUS is the acronym for Virtual European Music School, a project which seeks to design, develop, implement and evaluate a virtual educational environment destined for learning to play wind instruments: the flute, the saxophone, the clarinet, and the recorder. The platform addressed beginners and medium-level learners and proposed interactive methods for:

- individual practice, where the online evaluation of a student's performance was possible not only during the exercise, but also after its conclusion, due to a complete feedback;
- study in the classroom, offering support instruments for teachers in the process of teaching music in groups in the classroom. That was possible with the help of the automatic administration of the network resources of VEMUS, which enable the use of the wireless capacities of laptops or tablets for setting up peer to peer networks without the need for any special configurations;
- distance learning, the VEMUS platform offers a collection of music exercises and assignments, enable the improvement of students' skills, instruments for the creation of new content as well as means of communication and collaboration which enable distance tutoring activities and the monitoring of the students' progress.

By incorporating the three learning modes into an integrated educational environment, we sought to combine virtual activities and traditional ones, creating the technological and pedagogical premises for a virtual platform dedicated to students and teachers throughout Europe: the Virtual European Music School [11]. The VEMUS project was based on the field research and the platform developed during the IMUTUS project [12], an interactive learning platform. Dedicated to students aged 9-15, the platform was devised as a support for the teaching and learning process, supporting both independent and collaborative practice. It offers the possibility to play a piece, listen to a reference recording thereof, then to record student performances, and submit these for evaluation. Students are offered an evaluation of their own performance, in order to guide practice towards the elements that need correction. More specifically, VEMUS provides the possibility to practice on specific musical pieces and hear reference recordings. This project started from an organized survey that indicated the existence of a necessity for such an educational system since, according to the outcomes, 88% of the responding students have access to a computer at home, while 69% of them believe that the computer could assist them in studying music [13]. The description of this platform speaks about a virtual 'assistant teacher' concept for guidance when the student practices at home, giving additional feedback between sessions with the actual teacher.

VEMUS provides pedagogical tools for teachers based on the improvement of digital scores through graphic and audio annotations. The teacher can thus personalize the students' tasks by adding annotations in the score. Besides those, the teacher can make special annotations that are invisible to the student, thus selecting difficult passages that the VEMUS evaluation system can concentrate on.

The pedagogical approach of VEMUS is based on the concept of "extended music score" which offers new ways of feedback communication and improves the learning process. Feedback is accomplished by adding graphic shapes, text, emoticons, and audio annotations to the music score [14]. This approach includes various graphic representations of music performances displayed in the form of a feedback curve that runs parallel to the score. These enable the visualization of the student's performance and the explanation of such concepts as: attack, articulation, etc.

The VEMUS platform integrates a varied, rich content. It includes a repertoire of pieces and exercises, as well as non-interactive exercises concentrating on the quality of sound and warm-up exercises, devised by experts for each instrument. The expertise of theses teachers generated a musical material reflecting the international, as well as the local repertoire. According to the concept of VEMUS, the repertoire is organized on 5 main levels. On each level the repertoire is organized into lesson groups for a better characterization of the competences required for each element of learning. The evaluation procedure of VEMUS included schools in Sweden, Greece, Romania, and Lithuania, completed by validation activities in Estonia. In this way an evaluation procedure was contrived which used student groups in order to determine the effect of employing VEMUS in music education as compared to control groups.

During the project, the Romanian partner, specialized in designing software and in researching innovative educational techniques, subcontracted music institutions – AMGD and the Augustin Bena Music School – which performed and recorded the pieces in the software and subsequently tested its functionality with the assistance of teachers and students. An important issue consisted in evaluating the platform and offering a feedback from teachers and students on the impact of the software's inclusion in the individual instrument practice. We can summarize the benefits gained by the Romanian music institutions as follows:

TABLE III
SYNTHESIS OF THE ACTIVITIES

Project/goals	AMGD's tasks as subcontracting institution	Accomplishments
The VEMUS platform integrated innovative e- learning components for: a) a self-practicing environment with evaluation and feedback, b) innovative tools for teaching music in groups of students by supporting collaborative activities, c) a distance learning platform that couples a content repository with communication and progress-monitoring tools.	- to organize project dissemination - to create samplers for the recordings in the software (approximately 500 musical examples) - to conduct the inquiry for testing the VEMUS platform in Cluj (questionnaires interviews).	- endowment with equipment - organization in AMGD of 2 workshops in the field of IT attended by teachers from various institutions, - trips to meetings within the VEMUS project - connecting to a European network and setting up a local network, - the appearance of AMGD and the partner Music School on European television (Euro News coverage).

IV. E-VOCAL LEARNING

The „e-vocal" project was enriched by the collaboration of professional Viennese musicians and resulted in a platform that can be used by music universities, music schools and adult education centers interested in classical singing, facilitating the assimilation of a very consistent repertoire.

Due to the rich database created we sought both to increase the technical level and to overcome the problems linked to the assimilation of multiple styles in training a singer for stage performance. The goal was to facilitate the following technical elements: correct position, centering and breath control, mastering basic knowledge of sight reading a vocal score, correct performance of the vocal repertoire, clear articulation, achieving adequate dynamics. We started from the identification of the practicing requests of vocal materials and the explanation of a variety of styles: classic singing, musical theatre, contemporary music [13]. By downloading a video file of a music aria one can simulate a rehearsal in which the student is guided to sing the piece according to the indications and tempo of the virtual conductor. http://www.e-vocal.com

The learning programme E-vocal learning includes:

a. Videos with conductors (a video with piano and voice and one just with piano for each aria); this exercise involves cooperation with a conductor, highlighting the rigors and difficulties of each particular piece;

b. Language, phonetics, and rhythm exercises focusing on the necessities of text performance, practiced by uttering the verses to the music's rhythm. For Italian, this task was entrusted to an experienced prompter from the Vienna State Opera;

3. The on-line platform for the learning of a repertoire appropriate for various voice types: soprano, alto, tenor, bass;

d. DVDs for offline learning, so that the database may also be used when no internet connection is available; all conductors' videos and the mp3 verse files are available on the "Learning-DVDs for singers". There are 10 DVDs published by C. F. Peters (www.edition-peters.de) since 2009.

The E-vocal learning platform is an educational resource with the following features:

- attractive design and easy downloading of conductors' videos and of mp3 verse files, as well as easy notation-Plug-In installation;
- it is readily extensible and enables the facile addition of new multimedia learning and training materials;
- it enables the access of various user types: teachers, students, and administrators;
- it offers varied communication opportunities: forums, message sites, contact forms, newsletter;
- it keeps a learning log in order to follow the educational process and to assist the teacher in monitoring the student's progress.

All through its development, the project was supervised by an external evaluator and tested within the distance learning system of AMGD. By applying qualitative interviewing techniques we performed an analysis of the environment where the project took place and applied individual corrections in the students' progress or collective corrections in building the platform.

TABLE IV
E-VOCAL CONTENT

Project content	Trained human resource	AMGD's tasks/achievements
e-learning platform for singing comprising: conductors' videos, language and phonetic exercises to the rhythm of arias in the repertoire, DVDs with the project repertoire.	- approximately 120 students from AMGD -10 singing teachers - IT staff of AMGD's Distance Learning Department	- product testing by the students - access to a database of musical examples (accompaniment music) necessary to singers - the distance learning (singing) students and 10 teachers were signed up (for a limited time) on the e-vocal platform - the use of the platform in the distance learning programme as an educational resource

V. DIRECT IMPACT MULTIMEDIA APPLICATION (DIMA)

As an outcome of the collaboration in the above mentioned European projects, AMGD applied for a European financing through the entity named the Executive Financing Unit of Higher Education in Romania for a project that sought to integrate multimedia resources in music education. Due to this project we created a specially adapted e-learning platform comprising: training facilities, support in using and integrating ICT in a flexible curriculum, the thematic systematization of music terms in an on-line glossary of music terminology.

The teaching staff involved in developing the DIMA platform received training for creating, implementing, and using the resources on the DIMA platform and were offered specific guides on developing courses in e-form and on using the platform. These steps were preceded by an inquiry among the students enrolled in AMGD's educational programs, which showed that they were interested in using on-line educational resources. Students use the internet for accessing new information, thus motivating the necessity to create a database specific for the field of music:

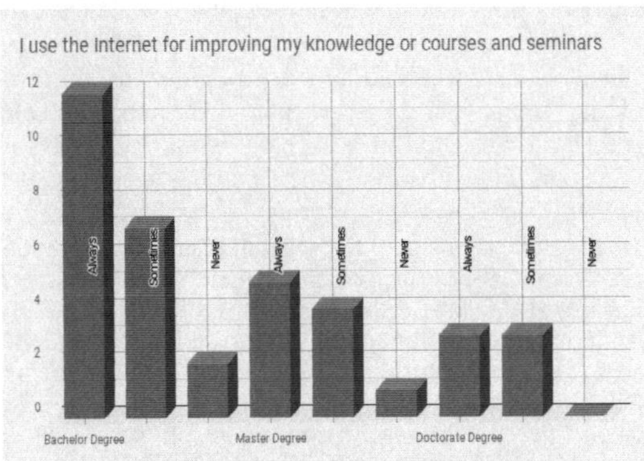

Figure 4. The level to which information is accessed on-line

There is a broad range of technologies that were used to address curriculum requests and to connect with other users.

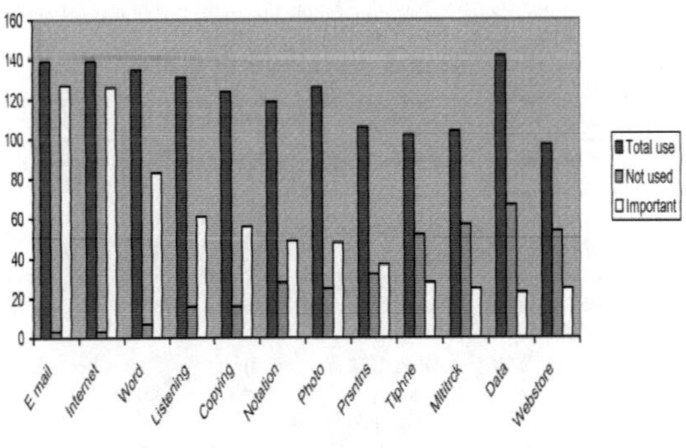

Figure 5. The type of technology employed

The surveys conducted in the Department of Distance Learning of the Academy of Music Gheorghe Dima in Cluj-Napoca revealed a series of issues linked to the students' needs of accessing educational materials and literature; however, the students expressed their desire to learn through information exchanges within the learning community and to get easier access to the curriculum content through on-line tutoring:

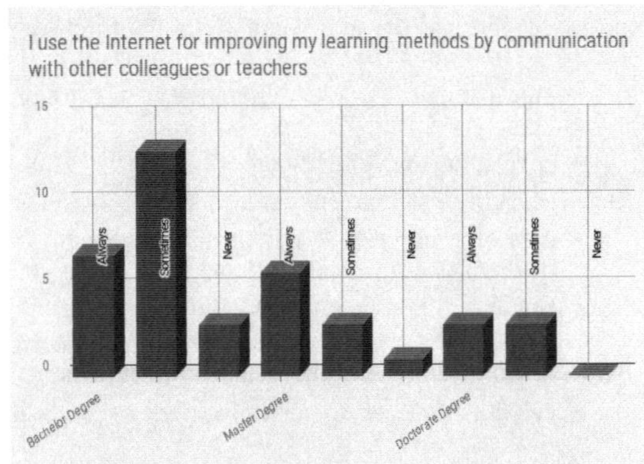

Figure 6. Assessment of the curriculum content presentation

The starting point of the project that created the distance learning platform was the requests expressed by the students, who were involved in drafting certain training materials on the platform and, along with an entity specialized in IT, the Ecological Informatics Society, had an active share in creating the electronic DIMA platform. The entire teaching staff of the academy contributed to the terminological glossary, so that the musical terms and expressions are now available in multimedia format on the platform dedicated to the distance learning programme (http://decid.amgd.ro/dima), where new multimedia terminology fields can be created for those who wish to contribute to the development of the existing database. The basic fund of the musical glossary comprises the following sections:

- Instruments and singing (keyboard, string, wind, and percussion instruments, singing), being made up of: scores, performance examples, audio and video examples, clues for technical solutions, stylistic incursions;
- Composers and music styles: systematizations according to stylistic stages, audio and video examples, scores, references;
- Musical theories and applications for such subjects as music theory, harmony, counterpoint, folklore, aesthetics, dramaturgy, by means of scores and audio/video/text examples;
- Information and communication technologies in music and presentation of reference points in electronic music technology.
- Theoretical guide for creating multimedia applications including: training in multimedia, Sibelius, and Audacity.

After the conclusion of the construction process of the distance learning system used in AMGD, based on an electronic platform with multiple functionalities, we created a system that enables us to monitor its use by means of a questionnaire for users (full-time and distance learning students, master students, doctoral students, as well as teaching staff). The questionnaire tested its usefulness, focusing on: competence in using on-line resources, access to electronic information and to computerized infrastructure, IT-supported methods of music education, learning mediated by accessible technologies, integration of multimedia resources into music education. The outcomes highlighted a significantly improved level of IT use by musicians: ICT is regarded as a tool to support teachers in accomplishing the following tasks:

- improving the lesson design through learning platforms;
- developing tools and resources;
- engaging and motivating students;
- providing opportunities for students to learn in alternative and challenging ways;
- enabling both collaborative and individual work;
- providing access to sources of information by searching educational websites on the internet;
- helping students to investigate new musical alternatives;
- helping students to review, refine, redraft and modify work;
- assisting students in refining their performances, compositional or learning skills.

TABLE V
SYNTHESIS OF DIMA OUTPUTS

Project	Achievements
DIMA -creating a multimedia platform (DIMA) -creating courses in multimedia format -editing a guide of good practice issued in electronic and classic form	-training the teaching staff in creating video/audio materials -creating a systemized database of musical terms -creating an international magazine called *ICT in Musical Field* -stimulation of scientific research by publishing articles and research papers by members of the project in specialized magazines/conferences

VI. CONCLUSIONS

The co-work in European networks resulted in the construction of our own distance learning system in AMGD [15]. and in finding solutions for a broad range of requests. In order to stress the practical relevance of collaboration within European networks, the gain in experience and the access to financing through European projects, we point out several of the benefits:

- The Prelude project offered: development of the teaching staff competence in IT, an imperative in the field of music, strengthening skills in using and even creating on-line teaching resources, assuring a wide access to informational resources (that is, to European platforms) and linking the Romanian music education system to the systems in other European countries [16].

-Using the VEMUS Platform relies on the active participation of music teachers, a base of activity that caused the construction of a local network between AMGD and music schools in the city. The interest shown by the children and parents who took part in the project demonstrated the opportunity of introducing ICT in music education in Romania.

-E-Vocal stimulated the use of multimedia resources, especially in the field of performance education, a field that is not easily accepted by specialists for on-line education. The examples of developing e-learning modules through MP3 multimedia formats and video learning systems, such as piano accompaniments, spoken texts of arias in their original language, or films with conductors, so as to offer students the occasion to learn from professionals' performances, and to participate in simulated rehearsals offered starting points in drafting AMGD's own multimedia anthology. The access to this platform consisting of recorded examples with renowned musicians of the Vienna Opera was initially free of charge for our students; it is currently used, in return for payment, by numerous students. They can interact, at home or at school, with the conductor, with singing techniques and with the musical and linguistic/phonetic characteristics of the arias.

In the DIMA project, the results of the preliminary inquiry confirmed the necessity of building a platform for the academy, as well as the need to render the educational content more accessible and to continue to organize training courses in IT, particularly for teachers. The platform that resulted meets the curricular necessities of AMGD, in on-line format, and, according to evaluations, improves the level of information assimilation, and stimulates the subjects' interest for accessing information.

As soon as the electronic platform of the Distance Learning Department became available, as a quality standard of the distance learning system, the students had access, through the offered facilities, to one of the most complex work instruments in the field of music, an on-line educational resource accompanied by a multimedia application called D.I.M.A. (Direct Impact Multimedia Application). This is an on-line terminology glossary for information and study that was implemented for and especially adapted to music education.

REFERENCES

[1] T.D. Chicioreanu, " The integration of e-learning platforms in the teaching activities", *ICTMF*, vol.VI, no.1, 2015, pp.7-17.

[2] N. Breeze, "Learning design and proscription: how generative activity was promoted in music composing", *International Journal Of Music Education,* vol. 27, nr. 3, 2009, pp. 204-219.

[3] C. Byrne and R.A.R. MacDonald, "The Use of Information and Communication Technology (I&CT) in the Scottish Music Curriculum: a Focus Group Investigation of Themes and Issues", *Music Education Research*, Vol. 4, No. 2, 2002, pp. 263-273.

[4] J. Mills, and A. Murray, "Music Technology Inspected: Good Teaching in Key Stage 3", *British Journal of Music Education,* Vol. 17, 2000, pp. 129–156.

[5] B. Crow, "Music-related ICT in education", in C. Philpott (Ed.), *Learning to Teach Music in the Secondary School*, London: Routledge/Falmer, 2001, pp. 135–162.

[6] J.R. Austin and M. Haefner Berg, "Exploring Music Practice among Sixth-Grade Band and Orchestra Students", *Psychology of Music,* Vol. 34, No. 4, 2006, pp. 535-558.

[7] E.Yung, N. Nedelcuţ, "Scalebook and Vemus, literacy software tool", *ICTMF,* vol.VII, no.2, 2016, pp. 37-42.

[8] M.Popean, "Cycling '74 Max, o platformă educaţională inter-curriculară", *ICTMF*, vol.VII, no.1, 2016, pp.7-17.

[9] P.R. Webster, "Computer-based Technology and Music Teaching and Learning: 2000–2005", *International Handbook of Research in Arts Education,* L. Bresler (Ed.), Springer, 2007, pp. 1311–1328.

[10] Y. Ju Joo, S. Joung, H. S. Son, "Structural relationships among effective factors on e-learners' motivation for skill transfer", *Computers in Human Behavior*, vol. 32, Issue null, 2013, pp. 335-342.

[11] D. Fober, S. Letz and Y. Orlarey, "VEMUS – Feedback and Groupware Technologies for Music Instrument Learning",

Proceedings SMC'07, 4th Sound and Music Computing Conference, Lefkada, Greece, July 2007, pp.117-123.

[12] S. Raptis, A. Chalamandaris, A. Baxevanis, A. Askenfelt, E. Schoonderwaldt, K. Falkenberg Hansen, D. Fober, S. Letz, and Y. Orlarey, "IMUTUS - an Effective Practicing Environment for Music Tuition", *ICMC-2005 Conference Proceedings*, pp. 383–Conference on Creativity & Cognition, April 2005, pp. 166– 175.

[13] J. Walding, "E-vocal com: e-learning in classical vocal training, an educational platform for singers", ICTMF, vol II, nr.1, 2011, pp 71-74.

[14] D. Fober, S. Letz, Y. Orlarey, A. Askenfelt, K. Falkenberg Hansen, and E. Schoonderwaldt, "IMUTUS - an Interactive Music Tuition System", *Proceedings of the SMC'04 Conference*, IRCAM 2004, pp. 97–103.

[15] N.Nedelcut, C.G.Pop, "The Electronic Platform – A Multifunctional Tool of Distance Learning", *ICTMF,* vol VI, no 2, 2015, pp. 39-48.

[16] "Prelude Training Programme on ICT in Music", Trainees' guide; Student Platform Manual; *Final report on teachers' needs analysis,* No. I129282-CP-1-2006-1-GR-COMENIUS-C2, unpublished.

AUTHORS

Nelida Nedelcuţ is with the Academy of Music "Gheorghe Dima", Cluj-Napoca, 400079, I.C. Bratianu street, Nr. 25, ROMANIA (e-mail: nelida.nedelcut@ amgd.ro).

Ciprian Gabriel Pop is with the Academy of Music "Gheorghe Dima", Cluj-Napoca, 400079, I.C. Bratianu street, Nr. 25, ROMANIA (e-mail: ciprian.pop@ amgd.ro).

Amalia Cristina Nedelcuţ is with the Babes-Bolyai University, Faculty of Economics and Business Administration/Management Department, Cluj-Napoca, 400591, Teodor Mihali street, Nr.58-60. ROMANIA (e-mail: amalianedelcut@gmail.com).

Manuscript received 12 March 2018.
Published as submitted by the author(s).

Design Science Research for Work-Integrated e-Learning

Christian Master Ostlund[1], Lars Svensson[1]
[1] University West /Department of economics and IT, Trollhattan, Sweden

Abstract— **The digitalization of work in all societal sector calls for flexible models for constant competence development of the workforce. This paper addresses the challenge of designing e-learning services that support continuous competence development of knowledge workers in the public sector. We present and discuss how four cycles of action design research informed the formulation of a nascent design theory for web lectures in the context of the Swedish Academy of County Administrations. Our work departs from a design theory on authentic learning developed and validated for K-12 education. Through our empirical work we have been able to adapt and transform the framework for authentic learning to fit the conditions of professional competence development in the public sector. The analysis has been conducted through a mixed method research approach where log data from e-learners are combined with interviews and observations. We conclude that a design theory for web lecturing should be based on 10 design guidelines that collectively frame the challenge of designing for e-training.**

Index Terms— **Design science research, Web lecture application, Work-integrated e-learning.**

I. Introduction

The nature of work is changing in all sectors of society, and due to, for instance, digitalization, robotization, and globalization there are constantly new demands on what it takes to stay competent within existing professions, and/or what competencies that need to be developed to meet the demands of new and emerging vocations and professions [1]. To a large extent organizations and individuals are looking at digital services and systems to provide flexible support for these challenges of competence development [2]. However, a majority of the research that informs the design of e-learning services are based on studies in a scholastic context, and as a consequence there is a risk that such design frameworks fail to grasp the situated needs that digital training of the workforce calls for.

This paper addresses the challenge of supporting continuous competence development of knowledge workers in the public sector. We present and discuss how four cycles of action design research [3] informed the formulation of a nascent design theory for web lectures in the context of the Swedish Academy of County Administrations. Our work departs from a design theory on authentic e-learning developed and validated for K-12 education [4]. Through our empirical work we have been able to adapt and transform the framework for authentic e-learning to fit the conditions of professional competence development in the public sector. The analysis has been conducted through a mixed method research approach where log data from e-learners are combined with interviews and observations. We conclude that a design theory for web lecturing should be based on 10 design guidelines that collectively frame the challenge of designing for e-training.

II. Design Science Research

Simon [5] first distinguished between exploratory/traditional science and the sciences of the artificial, i.e. how to design artifacts, already 1969. Around this time a tradition of design-oriented research grew strong in Scandinavia. It started in the early nineteen seventies when the Scandinavian unions demanded more influence over the new technologies that were being introduced in the workplace and affected the employees [6]. The Scandinavian tradition aimed at intervention through changing the work practice combined with the systematic collection and analysis of data [7]. It was also essential to not only contribute to research, but also to share the results and the experiences with workers and other workplaces.

In nineteen ninety Takeda et al., [8] wanted to develop a model to support the development of Computer-Aided Design (CAD) systems. The design cycle model consisted of five sub-processes: (1) awareness of the problem, (2) suggestion, (3) development, (4) evaluation, and (5) conclusion [8]. This design cycle was later used by Vaishnavi and Kuechler [9] when developing a method for DSR. During the same period Nunamaker et al., [10] presented a framework for using systems development as a methodology in IS research. Nunamaker et al., [10] argued that systems development and the testing and evaluation of systems under development very well could result in research contributions. Although Nunamaker et al. [10] did not reference Simon [5] or call it design science, it is a clear contribution to design science.

Walls et al., [11] on the other hand referenced Simon's [5] call for a science of the artificial when they presented a model for creating IS design theories. Walls et al., [11] listed seven characteristics that distinguished design theories, and proposed that IS design theories should be prescriptive so they could be used for solving practical problems. Markus et al., [12] later furthered the work of Walls et al., [11] proposing that IS design theories could be a set of user requirements derived from kernel theory, principles for the development process, and principles supporting the design of a system [12]. This system is meant to solve specific problems for certain situations, but design science research should also generate a solution for a class of problems. This generalization for a class of problems is meant to be used by both researchers and practitioners to solve other problems from the same class [13].

Gregor and Hevner [14] present a knowledge contribution framework for design science research project to help position the contributions of a design science research project. The framework has four dimensions with a solution maturity from high to low on one axis and application domain maturity on the other axis, also from high to low. This gives four types of knowledge contributions: improvement, invention, routine design and exaptation. An improvement is a new solution to an already known problem, whereas invention is a new solution to a new problem. Routine design is simply applying an existing solution to a known problem and is not considered to be a high knowledge contribution. However, if a known solution, e.g. from another field or domain, is applied to a new problem then that exaptation is considered to be a knowledge contribution.

In later years there has been efforts stressing that design science research does not need to be set up as a traditional experiment [3] as implied in many of the early research papers e.g. [11]. Baskerville, Pries-Heje, and Venable [15] state that by merging the common design science research process of "design, build-artifact, and evaluation" together with the iterative soft systems methodology, a better understanding of the problem is gained. Sein et al., [3] address the problem of traditional design science research not recognizing the impact of the organizational context on the development of IT artifacts by incorporating action research into design science research.

III. THE E-TRAIN CASE

The case organization was a national Swedish competence development network that involved all County administrations of Sweden. Together they had joined an initiative that aimed at collaborating on delivering e-learning modules that allowed specialist within the organization to design and deliver digital training for new employees that needed to be socialized into existing work practices, as well as providing support for organizational development in response to changes in legislation and other contextual drivers that called for new competencies in the organizations [16].

To develop these e-learning modules the iterative cyclical research process by Vaishnavi and Kuechler [9] was chosen. The first phase is an awareness of a problem. A suggestion for a solution to the problem is then derived from the existing knowledge base for that particular problem domain. This can be a conceptual model for a system or an early prototype. The system is then developed and implemented in the two following step. If the development is successful, the system is then evaluated in the next step. If the development or the implementation is unsuccessful, then the design research process is then cycled back to the awareness of problem phase, starting a new cycle with a better understanding on how to solve the problem. When the evaluation finally has reached a successful conclusion, then it is the end of the research effort and newly gained knowledge is written up and added to the existing body of knowledge within that problem domain. Another contribution in the form of a functional working system, is also the end result.

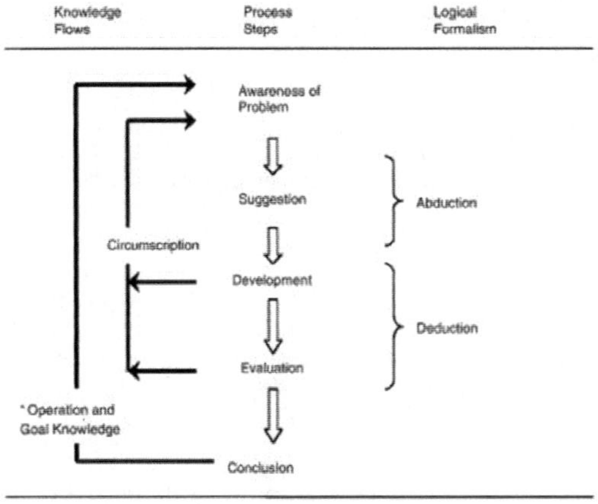

Figure 1. The Design Research Cycle [9].

A. *First Cycle - Test of a Pilot Concept*

Based on the design guidelines from an authentic e-learning framework by Herrington, Reeves, and Oliver [4] along with the design guidelines for digital resources and the GUI, a conceptual prototype was developed using Synchronized Multimedia Integration Language. Although after demonstrating the prototype it became clear that the application had to be re-designed so that the implementation did not demand the installation of new programs or plug-ins.

B. *Second Cycle - Exploring Usability and Work-Integration*

Since the county administration used PCs with Windows NT or XP, a new prototype using XHTML with embedded video was developed. The new design of the Web Lecture Application (WLA) was still based on the concept derived from the authentic e-learning framework in the first cycle. The new design contained embedded videos on how to search the WWW, a discussion board, information on how to contact the responsible teacher, and links to additional resources on how to search the WWW. The WLA was evaluated through an online questionnaire with the 15 respondents, one interview and web log data. The questionnaire and interview indicated that the majority of the users were satisfied with both the content and the WLA as a whole. But during the test period none of the learners had used the discussion forum. The reason for this was that they did not feel the need to collaborate or discuss the subject of the study with the other participants. When evaluated against the goal of authentic e-learning [4] this posed a potential problem. The problem was that collaboration promotes reflection and the discussion board was incorporated into the WLA to address that. The users still reflected since they stated in the evaluating that they all learned something new and all but one had changed the way they search the WWW after completing the web lecture. Even so, it could be argued that the learning outcome would be of more relevance, if the participants were encouraged and coached to collaborate and thereby reflect even more. In conclusion, the second cycle was a first test of how the use of the WLA could be integrated into the everyday work of the participants.

C. Third Cycle - Exploring Incentives and motivation for Collaborative learning

To address the problem with the unused discussion board, an assessing assignment was created, where a certificate was awarded upon conclusion. In the redesign of the WLA, the assessment module was based on peer-review and expert feedback. The assessment was twofold, one part where the employees received feedback from their peers and one part where they received feedback from an expert. The employee was to describe a search they had done relating to their work practice on which they would get expert feedback from the teacher. They should also comment on a description of search written by another peer.

This time the WLA was evaluated through an online questionnaire with 11 respondents and 10 interviews. None of the 20 participants chose to do the assignment. When asked about the reason for this the most common answer was lack of time and no real interest in a certificate. When asked about collaboration with other learners they felt no need for it, although some of the interviewees had discussed the content with nearby colleagues or members of their family. In conclusion, the third cycle demonstrated that incentives and motivation for training should not necessarily be designed to be mediated by IT, and local practices of reflection and discussion are supplements to mediated online reflection.

D. Fourth Cycle - Translating the design Concept

The findings from cycles one to three also informed the development of a WLA introducing employees at the county administration in all the counties to a new IT milieu. The authentic e-learning framework and the refinement of the authentic e-learning framework that was made for the new version of "searching the www" WLA was presented for the developing team leaders at the county administration academy. At the day of the implementation the employees was interviewed to evaluate the WLA. 18 interviews were made and the analysis of the interviews provided further input for the adaptation of the authentic e-learning framework. The fourth cycle demonstrated that the design concept of the WLA could be translated to other topics and content.

IV. Findings – A Nascent Design Theory for Work-Integrated E-Learning

A. Figures and Tables

Through the four cycles of design research presented above a nascent design theory [14] for work-integrated e-learning has evolved and matured. The cycles have generated eight design principles for workplace e-training. Three of these design principles emerged from the four design cycles, and five design principles originated from the kernel framework of authentic e-learning [4], and were either confirmed as transferable to the context of work-integrated e-learning or adapted to conform to the conditions of work-integrated e-learning in a workplace such as the county administrations of Sweden. The principle of authentic assessment has been excluded from the nascent design theory for work-integrated e-learning, since the empirical data from the cycles of evaluation could not validate its claims. In the below table the design principles are presented and explained.

TABLE I.
THE PRINCIPLES OF E-TRAINING THROUGH WEB LECTURES.

Design principle	Design guidelines
Principle #I (Emergent)	Design the e-training so it adheres to the limitations and opportunities of the organizational and infrastructural context to facilitate implementation and maintenance. In this way unnecessarily burdening the implementation process and the maintenance of the system are avoided. This is also to protect the employees from technical issues while interacting with the WLA.
Principle #II (Emergent)	Design to support for interruptive use, so that learners are supported in prompt repetition of previous use-sessions. Clear instructions regarding how to find various components is one of the factors that is rated as important to learners' success in online courses.
Principle #III (Adapted)	Design for explorative use so learners can create flexible and individual use-patterns. Having more than one set of learning materials is suggested to enhance the learning outcome. Similarly, access to multiple perspectives can help employees better understand and get a deeper understanding.
Principle #IV (Adapted)	Design to promote learners' reflections with peers in their local workplace context. This could be done by encouraging optional collaboration by e.g. providing guided discussion points.
Principle #V (Adapted)	Design for reflection and variation in participants' levels of expertise, so that scaffolding is integrated into the design. To encourage reflection, the authentic tasks and activities need to

	require decision making. This will force the employee to reflect on various solutions to a problem by reflecting in action [17].
Principle #VI (Confirmed)	Design for a learning environment that provides an authentic context through authentic activities and authentic tasks. This means that before the web lecture content is created the designer needs to learn about where and how the knowledge will be used. The designer of the learning content should also avoid over simplifying complex cases and situations but rather keep the complexity of the real work setting.
Principle #VII (Adapted)	Use experts that reflect the ethics and the culture of the organization as content providers. Employees learn through everyday work activities by observations or imitation while working with others (Billet, 2014). This can be utilized in e-training by engaging internal or external experts. The access to experts can also help strengthen the organizational culture through the sharing of narratives and stories and can even help inaugurate new employees to the organizational culture and "the way we work here".
Principle #VIII (Emerged)	Design for attention through gentle reminders to counteract procrastination. When taking on e-training at work, it is inevitable that the learners are divided between their work and daily routines and the learning activities. This suggests the designer should incorporate a discreet reminder system or push to the learning activities.

The nascent design theory for work-integrated e-learning aims at integrating authentic and relevant learning that translates into attitudes and increased skills/competencies for autonomous and self-regulated employees with their everyday work.

V. Discussion and Conclusion

This paper demonstrates how design science research methodology, through confirming, exapting and developing emerging design principles, is well suited for designing work-integrated e-learning as well as contributing to the body of research on work-integrated e-learning. The four cycles of design research rendered valuable insights regarding the special conditions that frame the challenge of designing for work-integrated e-learning. At the core of design science are the developing/building and justifying/evaluating cycles, which are preceded by a problem identification phase [13, 9]. The result of each cycle may refine the work-integrated e-learning system and if so the system is tested again until the system is ready for use. At this point new knowledge from the artifact and the design process should be added to the knowledge base concerning a delimited "class-of-problems" [3]. Thus there are two outcomes of design science: the knowledge contribution and the designed artifact. This makes a design science research approach suitable for designing work place learning solutions

Additionally, the research put further light on the complexity of designing for work-integrated e-learning. The intricate task of combining instructional design informed by sound learning theories with technological design informed by the knowledge domain of IS are a constantly ongoing challenge for researchers. The experiences from the four cycles conducted in the E-train project provide tentative evidence that a design science research approach is suitable for providing a structured framing when designing work place e-learning solutions. In conclusion, our research have suggested a set of strengths with a design science approach, namely:

- Several cycles of DSR in different organizational context provides a clear framing of the class-of-problem that the design theory aims at addressing
- DSR provides structured methods for evaluation and validation of Design Principles that involves both practitioners and researchers
- Resulting in a design theory with a set of actionable Design Principles, DSR-output provide guidelines for both researchers and designers of e-learning
- Design Principles that are rooted in kernel theories can be confirmed, rejected, adapted, but also new principles emerging from the empirical data.

We realize that the design theory for work-integrated e-learning derived from the e-train project at the present stage is in a nascent stage, and that it's generalizability need to be further investigated in future design science research.

References

[1] Östlund, C. (2017). *Design for e-training.* Copenhagen: Copenhagen Business School.

[2] Magnusson, M., Stahl-Falck, P., Svensson, L., & Sørensen, C. (2000). Know-how when no time: Forming a distributed community of practice. *In Proceedings of the 1st international conference on Knowledge Management: Concepts and controversies.* University of Warwick, Warwick, Great Britain.

[3] Sein, M., Henfridsson, O., Purao, S., Rossi, M., and Lindgren, R. (2011). Action Design Research, *MIS Quarterly, 35*(1), 2011, pp. 37-56. Erratum, ibid., 35(4), 2011, pp. 1099-1099..

[4] Herrington, J., Reeves, T. C., and Oliver, R. (2010). *A guide to authentic E-learning.* New York: Routledge.

[5] Simon, H. A. (1996). *The Sciences of the Artificial*: MIT Press.

[6] Bansler, Jørgen (1989). Systems Development Research in Scandinavia: Three Theoretical Schools, *Scandinavian Journal of Information Systems, 1*(1), Article 1.

[7] Spinuzzi, C. (2005). The methodology of participatory design. *Technical Communication, 52*(2), 163-174.

[8] Takeda, H., Veerkamp, P., Tomiyama, T., and Yoshikawa, H. (1990). Modeling design processes. *AI magazine, 11*(4), 37-48.

[9] Vaishnavi, V. and Kuechler, W. (2008). *Design science research methods and patterns: innovating information and communication technology*. Boca Raton: Auerbach Publications.

[10] Nunamaker Jr, J. F., Chen, M., & Purdin, T. D. (1991). Systems development in information systems research. *Journal of management information systems, 7*(3), 89-106.

[11] Walls, J. G., Widmeyer, G. R., and El Sawy, O. A. (1992). Building an Information System Design Theory for Vigilant EIS. *Information Systems Research, 3*(1), 36-59.

[12] Markus, M. L., Majchrzak, A., & Gasser, L. (2002). A design theory for systems that support emergent knowledge processes. *MIS Quarterly, 26*(3), 179-212.

[13] Hevner, A. R., March, S. T., Park, J., and Ram, S. (2004). Design Science in Information Systems Research. *MIS Quarterly, 28*(1), 75-105.

[14] Gregor, S., and Hevner, A. R. (2013). Positioning and presenting design science research for maximum impact. *MIS Quarterly, 37*(2), 337-356.

[15] Baskerville, R., Pries-Heje, J., & Venable, J. (2009). Soft design science methodology. *Proceedings of the 4th International Conference on Design Science Research in Information Systems and Technology*. Philadelphia, Pennsylvania, ACM: 1-11.

[16] Svensson, L. (2004). Challenges for work-integrated e-learning. *The Journal of Workplace Learning*, 16(8), 492-502.

[17] Schön, D. A. (1983). *The Reflective Practitioner - How Professionals Think in Action*. US: Basic Books, Inc.

HoloLens, Augmented Reality and Teamwork: Merging Virtual and Real Workplaces

Fernando Salvetti[1], Barbara Bertagni[1], Pierluigi Ingrassia[2], Fabrizio Lamberti[3], Francesco Strada[3], Gabriele Prattịcò[3], Antony Vitillo[3]

[1]Logosnet: e-REAL Immersive Simulation Labs, Houston, USA, Lugano, Switzerland, Torino, Italy

[2]Simulation Center in Medicine and Health Science SIMNOVA, Università del Piemonte Orientale, Novara Italy

[3]Department of Control and Computer Engineering DAUIN, Politecnico di Torino, Italy

Abstract—***Two projects are introduced: a cooperative game aimed at fostering behavioral, cognitive and meta-cognitive skills within organizations (Holo-Transportation), and a technical procedure aimed at saving lives (Holo-Defibrillation). e-REAL were the educational setting: an environment where physical and digital objects co-exist and interact in real time. Both the two projects were self-instruction learning simulation programs developed to maximize learning results, reducing instructor intervention and cost. Cascading and growing technical know-how about defibrillation were the main target of Holo-Defibrillation, while Holo-Transportation were aimed at empowering teamwork by fostering cognitive flexibility, emotional intelligence and self-awareness, as well as at honing the epistemic acumen related to reviewing ongoing processes and procedures, errors and alternative options.***

Index Terms—**Holo-Transportation, Holo-Defibrillation, Mixed Reality, Simulation, e-REAL.**

I. Projects' Objectives

Two projects are introduced here: Holo-Trasportation, a cooperative game aimed at fostering behavioral, cognitive and meta-cognitive skills within organizations, and Holo-Defibrillation, a technical procedure aimed at saving lives within healthcare.

Both the two projects were self-instruction learning simulation programs developed to maximize learning results, reducing instructor intervention and cost.

Microsoft HoloLens technology and other new AR caps were used, enabling users to interact with high definition holograms. Learners used natural gestures, body movements and spoken commands to perform their tasks, with virtual 3D objects anchored to the learning environment.

The projects' environment was e-REAL, that is the merging of real and virtual worlds: an environment where physical and digital objects co-exist and interact in real time. e-REAL enables a number of activities using gestures and spoken commands: it submerges learners in an immersive reality—context related—where the challenge at hand is created by sophisticated, interactive computer animation in 3D and holographic projections. In such a way, not only systemic understanding and situational awareness but also relevant cognitive aids are provided.

e-REAL is an environment where learners have to face challenging situations that require, in order to be appropriately managed and solved, an effective teamwork aimed at facilitating complex tasks by generating repeated loops of observation, decision, action, and re-evaluation. The success factors within e-REAL are the ability to communicate, negotiate and cooperate in order to translate the knowledge of what needs to be done into effective team activity[1].

II. Holo-Defibrillation

Providing an effective cognitive aid to both lay people and healthcare providers in Basic Life Support and Defibrillation (BLSD) procedures is a relevant educational goal in resuscitation.[2] A self-instruction learning simulation program was developed to maximize learning results, helping to enhance motor skills and the retention of cognitive knowledge, reducing instructor intervention and cost. Microsoft HoloLens technology was used, enabling users to interact with high definition holograms. The solution was developed as a mixed reality self-instruction training environment allowing assessment, using a standard low-cost CPR manikin to deliver tactile information. The manikin was "augmented" by interactive virtual environment reproducing realistic scenarios. Learners used natural gestures, body movements and spoken commands to perform their tasks, with virtual 3D objects anchored to the manikin and to the environment. We believe such a project is the first in the domain of BLSD.

Holo-Defibrillation is an interactive mixed-reality learning environment, providing learners with real-time feedback. In training mode, a self-instruction program is provided. After a short induction phase, users are guided through the sequence of actions required. Non-player characters (NPC) with different roles (by-standers, patient relatives, medical team members) deliver information or assist the trainee during the procedure. In evaluation mode, no guidelines are given, as the system only records and analyzes actions performed by the assessed trainee. MR techniques provide more interactivity and increase realism, by enriching the real world with digital information registered into the user's perception of the environment.[3,4,5,6]

In order to assess the prototypal system, we performed a qualitative evaluation with a user panel. At the end, participants were given a questionnaire asking them to rate a number of statements using a 5-point Likert scale (1: strongly disagree, 5: strongly agree).

Our test is ongoing: 23 users (4 doctors and 19 residents) participated in the early experiments by testing the application once in training mode and filling the questionnaire. All of them had previous BLSD training and never (or rarely) used an AR application. Results showed a general appreciation of the system (average rate 4.7), which was found pleasant (4.1) and easy to use (4). The cognitive load required to operate the HoloLens was minimal (1.8): users could focus on the BLSD procedure and on carrying out actions requested. Voice (4.4) and gesture interaction (3.8) were evaluated positively, although some hand recognition errors reduced the feeling of having the right level of control over the system (3.4). Virtual contents were found realistic (3.8) and the reduced field of view of the HoloLens was not perceived as a severe limitation (1.3). Participants judged the system as capable of providing a real benefit as a training tool (4.2) and to help them to be more effective (4.2).

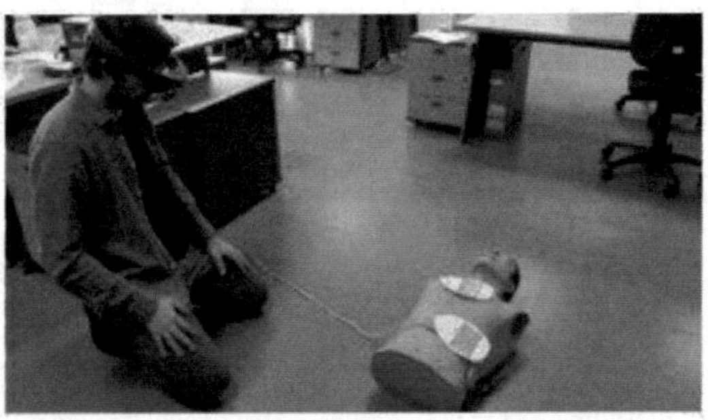

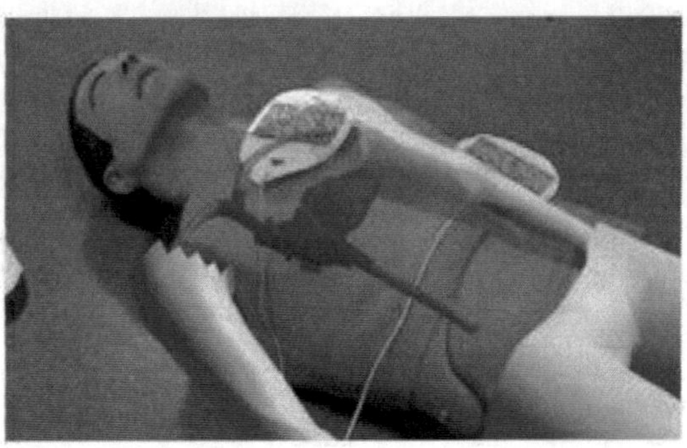

Our findings show that an interactive mixed reality learning environment could be an effective training tool for teaching BLSD procedures to both lay persons and healthcare providers. Holo-BLSD is a self-instruction learning program that requires minimal instructor intervention and, thus, can help to maximize learning results reducing the training cost. As major features, the system offers realistic haptic feedback through a CPR manikin and a virtual scenario that can be easily reconfigured to generate many different situations, including extreme and dangerous ones. All the data generated and the events occurring during the simulation (actions performed, NPC data, victim vital signs) are logged allowing instructors to immediately identify errors and difficulties of the trainees. Logging can also support an effective debriefing and, eventually, the creation of a library of training events. Future work will include a thorough assessment of both the training and evaluation tools proposed.

III. HOLO-TRANSPORTATION

Holo-Transportation is a cooperative game aimed at fostering behavioral, cognitive and meta-cognitive skills. A self-instruction learning simulation program was developed: deep spatial navigation is the simulated environment where 2 teams, comprised of minimum 2 people each, have to cooperate sharing information and knowledge relevant to navigate in the right way. The teams are in different places and can't directly look at each other: team wearing the HoloLens has to provide the most appropriate info to the other team, that has to manage the space navigation by the commands available on a big surface they are facing (part of an e-REAL interactive wall). Only in a few special situations the "drivers" are shown with images and recordings from the other team working with the HoloLens, sharing in such a way the same visual outputs.

Such a self-instruction learning simulation program was developed to maximize learning results, helping to enhance communication and knowledge sharing, as well as cognitive flexibility, uncertainty tolerance and the retention of cognitive information, reducing instructor intervention and cost. Microsoft HoloLens technology was used again, enabling users to interact with high definition holograms. The solution was developed as a Mixed Reality self-instruction training environment, allowing also self and team assessment.

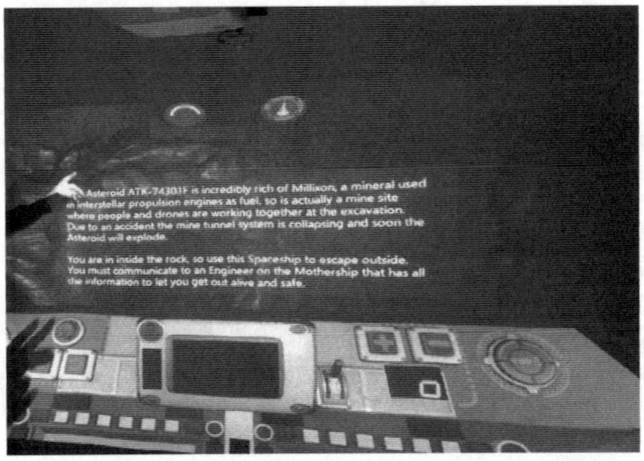

A self-instruction program is provided. After a short induction phase, users are guided through the sequence of actions required in order to perform deep spatial navigation. Mixed Reality techniques jointly with the e-REAL training environment provide more interactivity.

Learners are asked to make critical decisions, recognize a situation requiring rapid intervention, communicate and cooperate to share relevant information and knowledge, manage unforeseen events, deciding between parallel processing or performing one task at time in a sequence--taking into consideration critical contextual factors such as a lack of time, scarcity of resources and tools, previous impacting factors.

In order to assess the prototypal system, we performed a qualitative evaluation with a user panel. At the end, participants were given a questionnaire asking them to rate a number of statements using a 5-point Likert scale (1: strongly disagree, 5: strongly agree).

Our work is ongoing: 88 users (across industry: healthcare, energy, banking, etc.) participated in the early experiments by testing the application and filling the questionnaire. All of them never (or rarely) used an AR application. Results showed a general appreciation of the system (average rate 4.4), which was found pleasant (4) and easy to use (3.7). The cognitive load required to operate the HoloLens was minimal (1.8). Voice (4.8) and gesture interaction (4.8) were evaluated positively, although some hand recognition errors reduced the feeling of having the right level of control over the system (3). Virtual contents were found engaging (4) and the reduced field of view of the HoloLens was not perceived as a severe limitation (1.3). Participants judged the system as capable of providing a real benefit as a training tool (4.8) and to help them to be more effective (4.8).

Our findings show that an interactive mixed reality learning environment could be an effective training tool for enhancing team performance across industries. Holo-Transportation is a self-instruction learning program that requires minimal instructor intervention and, thus, can help to maximize learning results reducing the training cost. As major features, the system offers a virtual scenario that can be easily reconfigured to generate many different situations. All the data generated and the events occurring during the simulation are logged allowing instructors to immediately identify errors and difficulties of the trainees. Logging can also support an effective debriefing and, eventually, the creation of a library of training events.

Teamwork is a key target for soft-skills educators: soft and behavioral skills to enhance teamwork involve aspects of cognitive and social psychology, sociology and anthropology that have to be addressed in a proper way. Teamwork and cognitive collaboration from within an organization are probably two of the biggest factors that contribute to whether a firm succeeds or not. Formation of and communication between teams can often be beset with various issues that can stop a team's effectiveness dead in its tracks. Even more problematic is that the traditional formation of teams along the lines of functionality tends to create an unbalanced team that only has experience tackling the issues from one perspective, and is therefore unlikely to come up with 'outside of the box', innovative solutions.

Fostering cognitive collaboration both within and between teams means first understanding the people who make up those teams, knowing what their thinking and behavioral preferences are, and organizing them together in a way in which complements these different mental style.

From this approach to teamwork and team building derives a major benefit: a team that is balanced in different mental attributes has members who look at situations and communicate their ideas in different ways, leading to more varied solutions, which have been challenged and tested by those who view the situation differently. Individuals with differing behavioral preferences allow for a team to find an optimal way through cognitive collaboration to actually go about the challenge of solving issues and to communicate their solutions.

e-REAL is an effective setting to perform a number of tasks focusing on teamwork: learners are completely immersed in a 3D and holographic scenario where they can interact by natural gestures. The scenario integrates a wide range of challenging situations developed by visual storytelling techniques and delivered in an immersive (and interactive) way with tools tailored to provide feedback: so behavioral, cognitive and meta-cognitive aspects of performance are addressed and reviewed.

What today we know about learning from cognitive psychology is that people learn by practicing, with feedback to tell them what they're doing right and wrong and how to get better. The project's focus is about 8 specific key performance indicators: knowledge circulation and use of available information, effective communication, setting priorities and time keeping, workload distribution, stress management within the team (mainly when a fixation's error is occurring and detected), teamwork (mainly dealing with leadership and fellowship, power distance and cooperation). In such a way, by a teamwork activity it could be achieved a very relevant target: fostering cognitive flexibility, emotional intelligence and self-awareness, as well as honing the epistemic acumen related to reviewing ongoing processes and procedures, errors and alternative options.

Future work will include a thorough assessment of both the training and evaluation tools proposed.

REFERENCES

[1] www.e-real.net

[2] Spaite DW. Effectiveness of basic life support defibrillation. Annals of Emergency Medicine 1995; 25(5):697-8.

[3] Asgary A. Holodisaster: Leveraging Microsoft HoloLens in Disaster and Emergency Management. IAEM Bulletin 2017; January: 20-21.

[4] Christian J, Behringer R, Krieger H, Holzinger A, Moore D. Interaction Design of Augmented Education Environments. In: CAL 2011 Computer Assisted Learning (Learning Futures: Education, Technology & Sustainability), 2011.

[5] Pretto F, Manssour IH, Rodrigues da Silva E,Itaqui Lopes MH, Sarroglia Pinho M., Augmented Reality for Life Support Training. In: Proceedings of the 2009 ACM Symposium on Applied Computing (SAC), Honolulu, Hawaii, USA, March 9-12, 2009.

[6] Salvetti F, Bertagni B. Interactive Tutorials and Live Holograms in Continuing Medical Education: Case Studies from the e-REAL Experience. In: Proceedings of the ICELW Conference 2016, Columbia University, June 15th-17th, New York, NY, 2016.

[7] Bertagni B, La Rosa M, Salvetti F (Eds.), Learn How to Learn! Knowledge Society, Education and Training, Milan, Angeli, 2010; Bertagni B, La Rosa M, Salvetti F (Eds.), "Glocal" Working. Living and Working across the World with Cultural Intelligence, Angeli, Milan, 2010; Salvetti F, Bertagni B (Eds.), Learning 4.0: Advanced Simulation and Immersive Experiences, Interactive Infographics, Online Learning, Mentoring and Coaching, Angeli, Milan, 2018.

AUTHORS

Fernando Salvetti is with Logosnet and the e-REAL Labs (Turin, Italy; Lugano, Switzerland; Houston, USA).
Barbara Bertagni is with Logosnet and the e-REAL Labs (Turin, Italy; Lugano, Switzerland; Houston, USA).
Pierluigi Ingrassia is with the Simulation Center in Medicine and Health Science SIMNOVA, Università del Piemonte Orientale, Novara, Italy.
Andrea Bottino is with the Department of Control and Computer Engineering, Politecnico di Torino, Italy.
Fabrizio Lamberti is with the Department of Control and Computer Engineering, Politecnico di Torino, Italy.
Gabriele Pratticò is with the Department of Control and Computer Engineering, Politecnico di Torino, Italy.
Francesco Strada is with the Department of Control and Computer Engineering, Politecnico di Torino, Italy.
Antony Vitillo is with the Department of Control and Computer Engineering, Politecnico di Torino, Italy.

Manuscript received 15 March 2018. This work was supported in part by the U.S. Department of Commerce under Grant BS123456.

Published as submitted by the authors. Andrea Bottino, Pierluigi Ingrassia, Fabrizio Lamberti and Fernando Salvetti, Francesco Strada and Antony Vitillo are responsible for par. II; Fernando Salvetti, Gabriele Pratticò and Barbara Bertagni are responsible for par. III. Fernando Salvetti wrote also par. I

Applying a Threefold Gamification Approach in Software Engineering Education

Sigrid Schefer-Wenzl[1] and Igor Miladinovic[1]
[1] University of Applied Sciences, Computer Science and Digital Communications, Vienna, Austria

***Abstract*—Students of software engineering courses in higher education often experience a lack of motivation, partly caused by traditional teaching methods. In our study program we introduced a novel blended learning concept with threefold gamification elements for teaching software engineering. In this paper we present the teaching method mix with particular focus on the integration of three gamification elements to increase students' engagement.**

***Index Terms*—experiential learning, gamification, software engineering education.**

I. INTRODUCTION

Learning is known to be most effective when it is active, experiential, situated, problem-based, and provides immediate feedback [4]. These are properties that traditional software engineering courses in higher education often do not meet. A typical software engineering course consists of the following two elements: a lecture where concepts and theories are taught as well as small programming projects enabling students to apply this knowledge. However, lectures only allow passive learning and projects are very constrained, structured and well-defined, which does not prepare students adequately for their future jobs [11]. Moreover, using this setting, teachers of software engineering courses are often confronted with students' lack of motivation to continuously practice their programming skills (see, e.g., [5, 8]), which leads to high dropout rates as well as high failure rates in software engineering courses.

One promising approach to increase students' motivation is the introduction of gamification elements into software engineering courses. Gamification is defined as the application of game design elements to non-game activities with the goal to increase user experience and engagement [16]. Using gamification in different educational contexts is known to be one way to enhance learner motivation and to improve learning outcomes by capturing the interest of learners and inspiring them to continue learning [9, 10].

Our University of Applied Sciences Campus Vienna offers a Bachelor program in Computer Science and Digital Communications, with key skills focusing on a solid understanding of software development as well as comprehension of modern software engineering principles. One of the key lectures for those skills is "Software Engineering" in the third semester. Until now this course was taught using traditional methods, such as frontal lecture and home assignments. These methods were not able to support diverse entry levels of students frequently resulting in failing to achieve the learning objectives for students with lower entry levels. To address this issue we developed a new threefold gaming approach for teaching software engineering, supported by different gamification elements. In this paper we present this concept and discuss impacts of gamification on the achievement of learning objectives.

The remainder of this paper is structured as follows. Section II presents related work on gamification in software engineering courses. In Section III, we introduce our course design for a Bachelor-level course. In Section IV, we focus on the gamification concepts we employed in our course. Finally, Section V concludes this paper.

II. RELATED WORK

In recent years, several approaches have been proposed to motivate students and facilitate students' learning in the area of software development (see, e.g. [1, 2, 10]), some of them by using different kinds of game-based elements. Many authors discussing gamified software engineering courses state that students report improved content comprehension, retention and recap (see, e.g. [3]). This is mainly due to the practical application of the taught concepts in a game-based course.

Combefis et al. [8] analyzed several game-based online programming platforms. Amongst others they conclude that successful educational game platforms need to provide feedback and assessment, game elements need to be fun, and collaborative games and contests raise participation rates. According to Nah et al. [6], game design elements that are often used in an educational or learning context are experience points, levels/stages, badges, leaderboards, prizes/rewards, progress bars, storyline, and feedback.

Applying gamification to educational contexts has produced several promising results. However, a game-based approach is also associated with several risks. For example, Berkling and Thomas [5] introduced a gamification platform to teach a software engineering course. However, the results showed that students found the gamified environment as not being helpful, as they wanted to focus on relevant material for the exam.

Existing research in the field of applying gamification elements in software engineering education is still preliminary. More research on defining a systematic approach to design gamified learning activities, on relating learning goals with game-related methods as well as on evaluating the impact of gamification in software engineering education is needed.

III. COURSE DESIGN

A. *Learning Objectives*

We defined the following learning outcomes for our "Software Engineering" course:

- Understand and apply an effective software engineering process, based on knowledge of widely used software process models.
- Employ team working skills including organized planning, time management and inter-group negotiation.
- Capture, document and analyze requirements.
- Translate a requirements specification into an implementable design, following a structured process.
- Make effective usage of software design strategies.
- Design a testing strategy for a software system, employing techniques such as unit testing, test driven development and functional testing.
- Evaluate the final projects by checking compliance with the requirements, and analyze the design and implementation.

B. *Course overview*

The course consists of a lecture part and a tutorial part. The lecture part comprises the following four modules:

(1) Software engineering activities,
(2) Unified Modelling Language,
(3) process models, and
(4) invited lectures.

The software engineering activities module provides an overview of the main tasks of software engineering, such as requirements engineering, high level design, low level design, development and testing. The second module introduces Unified Modelling Language (UML) [12], enabling the students to graphically visualize the design of their future software projects. In the third part, different kinds of process models that structure the software development process are investigated and applied on smaller examples. The lecture part is completed with short lectures of four invited experts from several partner companies, who are involved in the software engineering process in their daily business.

During the lecture there are two example projects to illustrate how the learning content can be applied in practice. The first project is provided and presented by the lecturers demonstrating all aspects necessary for the implementation of the students' projects. The second project is elaborated by the students during the lecture to apply what they have learned on a simple project.

In the tutorial part, students work on a larger industry-like software gaming project, where they go through all software engineering phases according to a particular process model. Students are supported by the lecturers via regular coaching meetings.

C. *Applied Teaching Methods*

Figure 1 lists the applied methods for both, lecture and tutorial part. In the lecture we used blended learning to address different entry levels and learning patterns. The students prepare themselves for each lecture module with the provided learning material and generate control questions and corresponding answers in advance. The lecturers evaluate these inputs and select the most important questions to be discussed in the class. In-class sessions start with a recap of the learning content for this module, followed by a discussion on the selected questions. Afterwards, the obtained knowledge is applied on exercises in the context of the students' lecture projects.

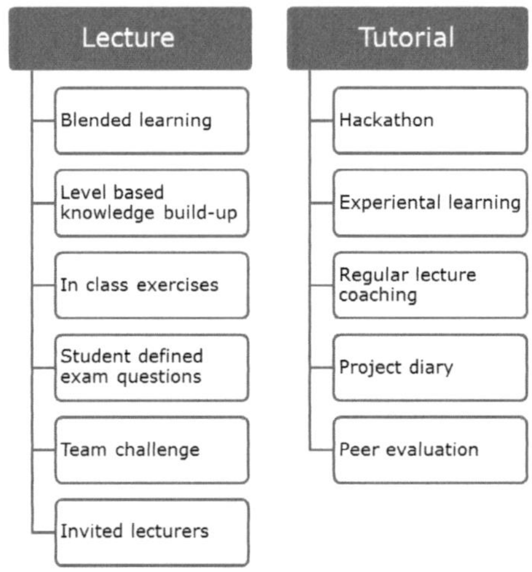

Figure 1. Method mix

In the tutorial part experiential learning via simulation of a real gaming software engineering project takes place. The whole tutorial is accompanied by regular lecturer coaching. The project starts with a Hackathon [13, 14] event, which is a six hours event where the students are brainstorming, discussing and evaluating their projects ideas. After the individual brainstorming phase there is a voting for each project idea by all students. One third of the ideas – those with the highest voting – are selected for the implementation. Each implementation is done in a group of three students with predefined roles: programmer, coordinator and designer. These roles have specified tasks and should reflect the roles of a real software project:

- The coordinator plans and documents the project, schedules regular meetings, keeps track of important decisions, talks with the customer, i.e. the lecturers, observes the whole development process and checks that all deliverables are provided in time.
- The designer defines the software architecture and the graphical user interface.
- The programmer is responsible for implementing and testing the project.

Students have to document their project progress in a project diary where they keep record of their decisions, agreements, findings, problems and successes. These project diary blogs are readable for all course members. Each course member can comment on the blog entries and give suggestions for improvements. Constructive comments are awarded with bonus points.

The final projects are evaluated in a peer assessment manner, where the compliance with the requirements specification and the high-level design is checked.

IV. Threefold Gamification

To foster the motivation of students even more, we introduced three gamification concepts in our lecture: a challenge, a level based progress tracking and experiential learning through own game projects.

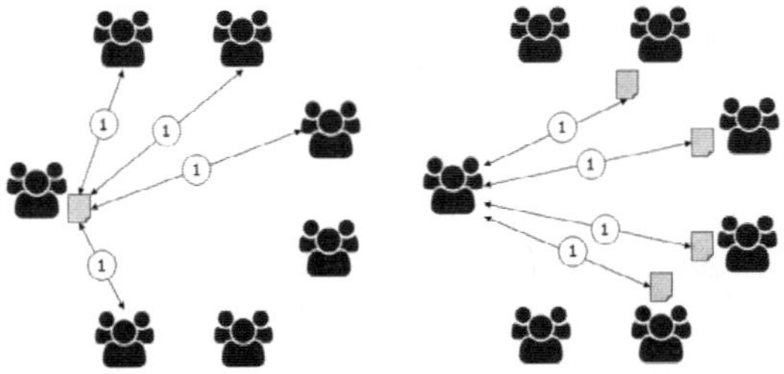

Figure 2. Team challenge

A. Challenge

The challenge is organized as a kind of competition between the development teams, where they compete for common resources, which are points for the grading in our lecture. The challenge applies for the requirements engineering and the high level design exercises of the lecture. Each group specifies these two documents for a given project (same for all the groups) and shares these specifications with a certain number of other groups (n). These groups challenge shared documentations and look for weaknesses in them. If no weaknesses are found, the group which owns the documents gets one grading point. Otherwise, the group which challenged the document gets that point. Figure 2 illustrates this process.

The total number of grading points which are achievable by this challenge can be adjusted by the number of groups which challenge the documentation. For each document – and there are two in our course – the maximum number of points is 2n-2.

B. Gaming Levels

The second gamification concept is based on knowledge levels according to Bloom's Taxonomy [15]. For our course we adapted the six original categories into four levels, as shown in Figure 3.

For each level we defined clear tasks and achievements to accomplish. The first level is Remember and Understand and the achievements are determined by a written examination. The Applied level is driven by lecture exercises deepening the theoretical knowledge and by self-created questions and answers about the lecture contents. The described challenge covers the Analyze and Evaluate level. Finally, the design and implementation of the own project in the tutorial part enable the students to move to the Create level.

When the students obtain at least half of the possible achievements from one level, they are promoted into the next level. This promotion is a precondition for achievements in the next level.

C. Experiential Learning

Simulating real-world projects is aimed to provide students with the experience in order to unify the practical understanding with the theoretical knowledge [10]. In our course, students are supposed to learn by experiencing all phases of a typical industry-like software project. They create a project idea and follow it until successful implementation. Therefore, students are likely to identify themselves with their projects resulting in an increased motivation. Applying the gamification concept here we intend to foster student engagement even more.

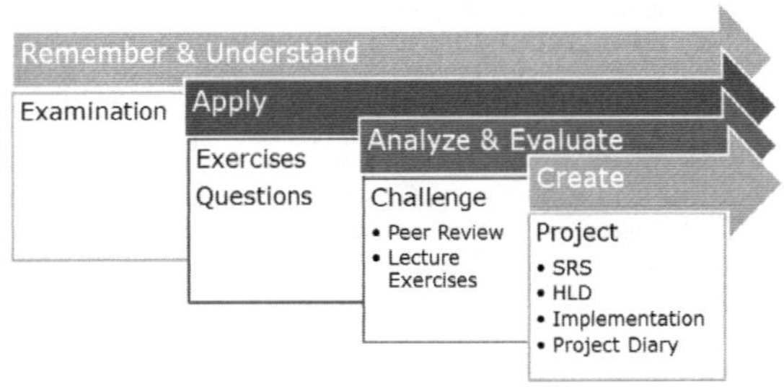

Figure 3. Knowledge levels

During the Hackathon event, students have to propose ideas for a project, which should be a gaming application. The best ideas are selected for implementation as described in Section III.C. Gaming applications have several advantages: A game needs clearly defined rules which constitute the requirements of the application. In addition, in a game functionality, design and performance are all important motivating the students not to neglect one of them. Usually games also frequently need a local database and cloud architecture which increases learning effects.

V. Conclusion

Different studies show that gamification can increase students' engagement in higher education. We designed a bachelor level software engineering course by combining a method mix with threefold gamification elements, *challenge*, *gaming levels* and *experiential learning*. With this concept we gradually address all the knowledge levels according to Bloom's Taxonomy. In future research, we will apply and evaluate this course concept in different student settings.

References

[1] A. Pears, S. Seidman, L. Malmi, L. Mannila, E. Adams, J. Bennedsen, M. Devlin, and J. Paterson, "A survey of literature on the teaching of introductory programming", In: *Working Group Reports on ITiCSE on Innovation and Technology in Computer Science Education, ITiCSE-WGR '07*, pp. 204–223, Dundee, Scotland. ACM, 2007.

[2] A. Vihavainen, J. Airaksinen, and C. Watson, "A systematic review of approaches for teaching introductory programming and their influence on success", In: *Proceedings of the Tenth Annual Conference on International Computing Education Research, ICER '14*, pp. 19–26, Glasgow, United Kingdom. ACM, 2014.

[3] P. G. F. Matsubara, C. L. Correa da Silva, "Game elements in a software engineering study group: a case study", In: *Proceedings of the 39th International Conference on Software Engineering: Software Engineering and Education Track, ICSE-SEET '17*, pp. 160-169, Buenos Aires, Argentina, IEEE Press, 2017.

[4] E. A. Boyle, T. M. Connolly, T. Hainey, "The role of psychology in understanding the impact of computer games", In: *Entertainment Computing*, vol. 2, nr. 2, 69–74, 2011.

[5] K. Berkling, C. Thomas, Gamification of a Software Engineering Course and a detailed analysis of the factors that lead to it's failure. In: *Proc. Of the International Conference on Interactive Collaborative Learning*, pp. 525–530, Kazan, Russia, IEEE Press, October 2013.

[6] F. F.-H. Nah, Q. Zeng, V. R. Telaprolu, A. P. Ayyappa, B. Eschenbrenner, "Gamification of Education: A Review of Literature", In: *Proc. of the International Conference on HCI in Business, HCIB 2014,* Heraklion, Crete, Greece, Lecture Notes in Computer Science, vol 8527, Springer, pp. 401-409, June 2014.

[7] D. J. Frailey, "The times, they are changing", In: *Software Engineering Education and Training*, pp.1-2, Klagenfurt, Austria, 2014.

[8] S Combéfis, G. Beresnevicius, V. Dagiene, "Learning Programming through Games and Contests: Overview, Characterisation and Discussion", In: *International Olympiad in Informatics*, vol. 10, pp. 39–60. Vilnius, Lithuania, 2016.

[9] G. Barata, S. Gama, J. Jorge, D. Goncalves, "Improving Participation and Learning with Gamification", In: *Proc. of the 1st International Conference on Gameful Design, Research, and Applications*, Toronto, Ontario, Canada, 2013.

[10] M. Kosa, M. Yilmaz, R. O'Connor, P. Clarke, "Software Engineering Education and Games: A Systematic Literature Review", In: *Journal of Universal Computer Science*, vol. 22, no. 12, pp. 1558-1574, 2016.

[11] Souza, Mauricio R. et al., "A systematic mapping study on game-related methods for software engineering education", In: Information and software technology, vol. 95, March 2018.

[12] Object Management Group, "Unified Modeling Language (UML). Version 2.5.1". available at: https://www.omg.org/spec/UML/2.5.1/, Dec. 2017.

[13] B. Rosell, S. Kumar, and J. Shepherd, "Unleashing innovation through internal hackathons", In: *IEEE Innovations in Technology Conference*, pp. 1–8, May 2014.

[14] E. H. Trainer, A. Kalyanasundaram, C. Chaihirunkarn, and J. D. Herbsleb, "How to hackathon: Socio-technical tradeoffs in brief, intensive collocation", In: *Proceedings of the 19th ACM Conference on Computer-Supported Cooperative Work & Social Computing*, CSCW'16, pp. 1118–1130, New York, NY, USA, 2016.

[15] B. S. Bloom, "Taxonomy of educational objectives, handbook I: Cognitive domain.", New York: David McKay, 1956.

[16] S. Deterding, D. Dixon, R. Khaled, L. Nacke, "From game design elements to gamefulness: defining 'gamification'". In: *Proceedings of the 15th International Academic MindTrek Conference: Envisioning Future Media Environments*, Tampere, Finland, September 2011.

AUTHORS

Sigrid Schefer-Wenzl is a senior researcher and lecturer at the University of Applied Sciences Campus Vienna, Austria (e-mail: sigrid.schefer-wenzl@fh-campuswien.ac.at).

Igor Miladinovic is head of the degree program Information Technologies and Telecommunication at the University of Applied Science Campus Vienna, Austria (e-mail: igor.miladinovic@fh-campuswien.ac.at).

Manuscript received 15 March 2018.

Published as submitted by the author(s).

The Design and Development of a Mobile Phone Application for STEM based on a Novel Engineering Approach

Yaoxian Zhuang, Liyan Wang, Feng-Kuang Chiang[1]
[1]Department of Educational Technology, School of Education
Shanghai Normal University, China

***Abstract*—STEM education provides students with interdisciplinary knowledge to improve problem-solving ability. The purpose of this study is to explore whether students could achieve the goal of STEM education by mobile learning. This study developed a mobile application which was named *Borrowing Your Enemy's Arrows* to support mobile learning about science, technology, engineering, and math (STEM). According to the textbooks for Grades 5-7, the teaching content of the APP was designed to help students get a better grasp of teaching contents and to help teachers save time in preparing classes. The central narrative, like cartoon or the dialogue of cartoon is used for APP to bridge the teaching contents. Therefore, learners can construct a real-life situation by App. To inspire learners' interest in STEM courses, the APP used games to test how well students did in learning. A shipbuilding task with the narrative background was set to improve learners' skills and interest in engineering learning. The educator could make the assessment of learners based on all their performance in the process of learning, including the design sketches, final products, the messages from students and the grade of game. For the purpose of improving the APP, teachers and students were interviewed to investigate users' feedback in this study.**

***Keywords*—STEM education, mobile learning, novel engineering**

I. INTRODUCTION

By integrating STEM education in science, technology, engineering, and mathematics, students can see the connection of knowledge between dispersed disciplines. By designing good STEM thematic activities, it is possible to increase students' interests and achievements in related disciplines [1]. However, since STEM education is multidisciplinary, it often takes a lot of time to develop a STEM course. This will prolong the student's study time, and will not achieve the goal of reducing the burden on students. What is worse, it will cause both students and teachers to feel impatient [2]. In the process of improving the STEM curriculum, some scholars have successively used mobile devices as teaching tools to guide students in autonomous exploration through mobile phones or tablet computers.

In previous studies, many scholars have developed APPs suitable for STEM learning to assist students in learning. Some Italian scholars have developed an application based on artificial intelligence. In the VLE (virtual learning environment), several students form a group and learn through role-play in the style of 3D images. Students in this learning environment will be more interested in participating in the course [3]. In the Science Center, with the help of the staff of the venue, the researchers selected the teaching content and reorganized students into multiple themes. The learners took mobile device to learn. Not only can they get timely feedback, but they can also learn the science center's fusion of STEM. Knowledge and attention are also more concentrated[4]. Digital game-based learning methods have been proved useful in improving students' enthusiasm and promoting learning in a technologically enhanced environment [5].

In order for learners to maintain a sustained focus on STEM courses, stories and novels are often used as one of the forms to guide curriculum progression. The novel engineering integrates engineering education and literacy in school-based curriculum in a new way. When students read materials (such as stories, novels, etc.) in a literature class, the characters in the novel or story will encounter some problems. Based on the situation of the story, the students can use their own knowledge and skills to complete the engineering design in collaboration with the team and with the support from the teacher to help the story characters solve the problems [6]. Wilson-Lopez and Gregory [7] pointed out that literacy instruction can be used to think deeply about engineering problems at various stages of the design process. Literacy and engineering are complementary and mutually reinforcing. The way the students design activities when they practice engineering can help them become more experienced readers or writers. Students apply reading comprehension strategies to engineering projects to help them become thoughtful engineers. Through the problems encountered by the characters in the novel, digging out the STEM elements among them makes it possible for the learner and the protagonist to overcome the difficulties and make the course more interesting and more persuasive. Therefore, the purpose of this study is to design and develop a mobile phone application which is called *Borrowing Your Enemy's Arrows* for STEM based on a Novel Engineering Approach.

Borrowing Your Enemy's Arrows was implemented with seventh-grade students from a junior high school of Jiaxing, China in March 8, 2018. This research study describes the design of *Borrowing Your Enemy's Arrows* and the results of recording-based interviews of six students and four teachers who had at least five years in their respective fields. We analyze these interviews to address the following three research questions:

RQ1: Is the design of *Borrowing Your Enemy's Arrows* reasonable?

RQ2: Is *Borrowing Your Enemy's Arrows* popular with seventh-grade students?

RQ3: How do you think to improve *Borrowing Your Enemy's Arrows*?

II. Design of Mobile Learning Games APP

The serious educational games can promote scientific practice and flow experience [8] so the teaching content of *Borrowing Your Enemy's Arrows* was based on the sixth- and seventh-grade teaching materials which is published by Shanghai Education Publishing House in order to foster STEM knowledge and skill (see Table 1). The novel project could help students who were afraid of science and engineering disciplines to overcome psychological barriers in order to improve students' interest in learning and participation, and help students who were not interested in Chinese learning to improve their literacy by solving engineering problems [6]. In the game of educational APPs, it was necessary to design clear knowledge instruction and practice to make the game more effective [9], and the test of knowledge was more helpful to students' mastery of knowledge than practical application [10]. In educational games, clear goals, immediate feedback, and appropriate difficulty were preconditions of flow [11].

A. *Description of the Game APP*

TABLE 1

List of Knowledge in *Borrowing Your Enemy's Arrows*

Subject	Knowledge	Contents
Science	Gaseous, liquid and solid	The formation of fog
	The effect of force	Deformation of the arch
	Friction	Rolling log
	Buoyancy	Floating boat
	Action and reaction	Wind-blown boat
History	The history of the ship	Ancient ship and modern ship
	The history of the Three Kingdoms	
Chinese	Time	Ancient time and modern time
	Peculiar language of character	
Engineering	The structure of the ship	Shipbuilding

Borrowing Your Enemy's Arrows is a serious mobile educational game played with Android mobile devices out of the junior high school. It was designed with Photoshop and developed with APP inventors. The design of interface and character were original.

The content of game APP is divided into five modules: Guide (guide to how to use); Cartoon (knowledge, story background); Think tank (list of knowledge); Shipbuilding (hands-on); Athletics (test). The players gained knowledge through cartoons, and then they built ships and played games. When they encountered difficulty, they could enter Cartoon to relearn or enter the Think Tank to summarize important knowledge (see Figure 1).

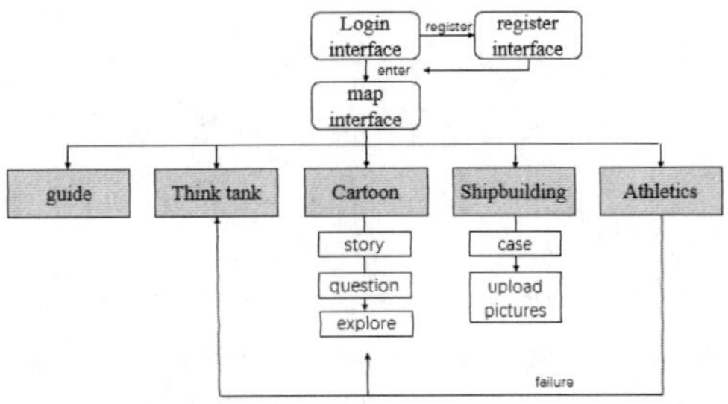

Figure 1. The Structure of *Borrowing Your Enemy's Arrows*

B. Cartoon

Borrowing Your Enemy's Arrows used a central narrative to link every module together. The core narrative was a story taken from one of China's best-known books *The Romance of the Three Kingdoms* by Luo Guanzhong. This is an episode from the Three Kingdoms. Zhou Yu ordered Zhuge Liang to manufacture 100,000 arrows within ten days, a mission almost impossible, with the hidden purpose of punishing Zhuge Liang in case that Zhuge Liang can not fulfill the task on time . Zhuge Liang rode boat to the enemy' s camp for making them believe surprise attack to shoot arrows. Zhuge Liang collected arrows by the scarecrows. The story is presented by comic so the students will be more interested and the relevant questions are set to promote students' thinking(see Figure 2).

Figure 2. Screenshot of a Cartoon

C. Shipbuilding

In the story of Cartoon, Zhuge Liang needed 20 ships, and thus *Borrowing Your Enemy's Arrows* demanded players to build ships. The task design of the game should follow the small step principle and accord with the requirements of the "zone of proximal development"[12].The virtual character will guide the students through the small tasks step by step. (see Figure 3). And the players were asked to upload a sketch of the design, a picture of artifacts, and their note-taking sheets that were scanned into the devices during the production process in order to evaluate students from different dimensionality.

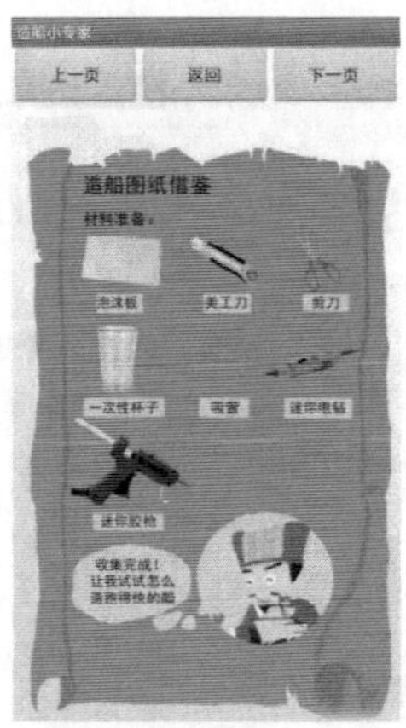

Figure 3. Screenshot of a Shipbuilding that Receives Hints during Gameplay

D. Athletics

The background of the Athletics was the story in Cartoon, and the players played games by role-playing for promoting the engagement. The goal of the game is to borrow 100,000 arrows from Cao Cao. Every time when the player is out of cards, the Athletics would display the number of arrows which the player had borrowed to make the player define the progress of the task (see Figure 4). When the player is at fault, the mobile phone vibrates to provide negative feedback and when the player wins the game, the mobile phone would sound a note of congratulation for the player, more specifically the sound of a firework display, to provide positive feedback.

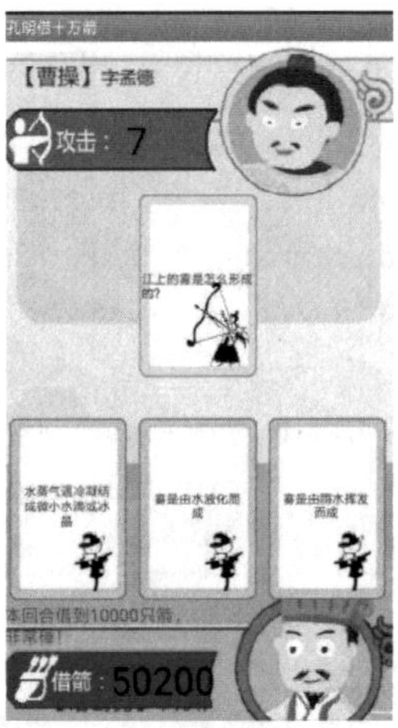

Figure 4. Screenshot of a Athletics

III. Methods

A. Setting and Participants

A sample of 6 seventh-grade students and four teachers was obtained from a junior high school in Jiaxing, China. The school had not a course about STEM or engineering. The 6 students included 3 male and 3 female students and every gender included high, middle and low grades. The 4 teachers who were at least five years in their respective fields included a computer teacher, a history teacher, a Chinese teacher, and a science teacher.

B. Study Design and Data Collection

This study employed qualitative research method. Date sources included: interviews, field observations, screen recording and the scores of the Athletics.

(1)Interviews

Students and teachers were assigned to play *Borrowing Your Enemy's Arrows* for half an hour. Immediately after it was completed, students and teachers participated in the interviews. The interview protocol of the students (see Table 2) included questions about TAM, flow experience, the overall design of the software and the attitude towards the software. Whereas the questions about flow experience were removed from the interview protocol of the teachers. All the interviews were audio recorded and later transcribed by the researcher.

Table 2. The Interview Protocol of the Students

	Dimensionality	Questions
TAM [13]	Perceived usefulness	When you use this APP, have you encountered any problems?
	Perceived ease of use	By using this APP, do you think it is useful for your study? What knowledge have you learned?
Flow experience [14]	No fear of failure	What do you do when you fail?
	Time distortion	Do you think time passes quickly than you realize in the process of using the APP? Do you want to play with it again?
	Loss of self consciousness	Field Observations
	Focused attention	
The overall design of the software.	Module design	What do you think of the modules in the software: Comics, Athletics, Shipbuilding, Think Tanks? Which are you most interested in? Which do you think needs to be improved? Please elaborate your suggestion.
	Art Design	What do you think of the art of software, or do you think it looks good in the software? Where do you think the artists need to change?
	Interaction	Do you think you can get clear and immediate feedback when you use the software? Do you find the interaction in software interesting?
	Teaching content	Do you think the knowledge involved in the software is difficult?
Attitude [15]	Degree of affection	Do you like this software?

(2)Field Observations

Two researchers conducted field observations during gameplay by following players. The researchers recorded observations about students' attention and expression to show the flow experience of the students especially in terms of focused attention and loss of self-consciousness.

(3)Screen Recording and the Score of the Athletics

When the students were using *Borrowing Your Enemy's Arrows*, the screen-recording software recorded the students' operation. And one researcher kept the score of the Athletics by watching screen recording.

IV. RESULTS

A. *The Score of the Athletics*

Table 3 presented the score of the Athletics in the screen recording. When the cartoon and the Think Tank were finished for the first time, the students did not complete the task, but most of them were able to complete the task at last. This indicated that the difficulty of the Athletics is appropriate. And the study found that when students failed their first try in the game some of them would go to Cartoon to review or go to Think Tank to learn or do both for a second time. Different choices were available to individuals (The full mark is 11).

Table 3. The Score of the Athletics

Student	Gender	Age	Ranking of the School/(N=500)	First Score	Last Score
S1	Female	13	1/500	8	11
S2	Female	14	232/500	8	10
S3	Female	13	411/500	4	8
S4	Male	13	250/500	6	11
S5	Male	14	39/500	8	11
S6	Male	14	451/500	7	10
mean		13.5	230.6/500	6.8	10.2

B. *Interviews*

(1)Technology Acceptance

Students could use the APP easily even without teacher's guidance. They thought that there was no problem with APP usage. Only one girl had a problem with the button, and she thought the problem was with the phone. However, teachers had demanded better APP usage, especially the computer teacher. Below, the computer teacher describes the problems during using the APP:

I can play it by myself, but some buttons are too small to recognize at first. Of course, the Icon of the Guide is also so small that I think it is just a picture. So I think you can put it in the middle of the map. And sometimes the button is malfunctional.

(interview, computer teacher, seven years' teaching experience)

In this APP, students and teachers agreed on that it could promote students' learning. And they were all aware that this is an interdisciplinary education software, but most people could only recognize science, history and language.

(2)Flow Experience

Most students could have flow experience. They didn't fear failure and thought time passed quickly. They wanted to play it again. On the other hand, five students focused on the APP and one student was distracted when the researchers were taking pictures and walking.

(3)The Overall Design of the Software

For the most impressive module, different people had different answers. Students prefered Shipbuilding and Athletics. Teachers' choices were much more dispersed since all four modules were mentioned. For the artistic designing, the requests of the girls were generally more than boys. Girls thought the image of the characters could become more exquisite. Computer teacher put forward her own ideas for the interaction of the Cartoon:

Cartoon is more attractive, but the interaction of the Cartoon is too easy. You can increase the frequency of interaction. For instance, when you touch on the characters, words and sounds then appear.

(interview, computer teacher, 7 years' experience)

For the teaching content, researchers asked the students about the difficulty and asked the teachers about its reasonableness. Students thought the difficulty of knowledge was appropriate, because the teaching content had the knowledge they had learned and the knowledge quite unknown to them. The teacher thought the content was accurate.

(4)Attitude

The students' attitude was positive. They thought the APP was very interesting, and they would like to recommend it to their friends. However, the teachers' attitude is more complex. Some teachers thought that this was a useful tool for the students. Other teachers thought that the phone could disturb the students' study and cause other problems. The teacher of Chinese subject describes the problems of APP as below:

You should consider which teacher can teach this curriculum. Now none can teach it in our school. And the app just has a story, so the curriculum is just one. It's too little.

(interview, teacher of Chinese, 20 years' experience)

V. Discussion

This paper described a mobile phone application for STEM based on a novel engineering approach to foster STEM knowledge and skills. In this study, researchers introduced the design of *Borrowing Your Enemy's Arrows* and implemented a simple user evaluation in order to find out whether the mobile phone application design was reasonable, whether the teaching content was accurate, and how to improve it.

As a whole, the teaching content of *Borrowing Your Enemy's Arrows* is accurate and conforms to the content of the textbook. The design of *Borrowing Your Enemy's Arrows* is reasonable and has the following advantages. First, *Borrowing Your Enemy's Arrows* based on a novel engineering approach created a problem-based learning environment to promote students' learning. Second, the method of evaluation was diverse, both competitive and practical. Third, students could personalize their learning based on different knowledge types.

Of course, there were some deficiencies in *Borrowing Your Enemy's Arrows* that needed to be improved. First, add story content, design a series of curriculums to support systematic teaching. Second, increase the forms of interaction and increase the chance of human-computer interaction. Third, improve the design of both the character and the interface to increase visual aesthetics.

VI. Study Limitations

In this study, a STEM educational software on the basis of novel engineering was developed. After interviewing students and teachers, the results showed that the software could stimulate students' interest and help them learn STEM contents better. However, there were still some limitations. In the study, we only had six samples. Due to the limited time of investigation, the subjects failed to complete the engineering module and further investigation on subsequent memory wasn't able to be carried out.

In addition to the fact that STEM type apps could help improve students' learning motivation, they also had a positive effect on guiding students to complete STEM contents. However, researchers still needed to develop learning materials to go with the APP (e.g., textbooks, courses, video, toolkit) to support students in learning STEM contents.

References

[1] Moreno, N. P., Tharp, B. Z., Vogt, G., Newell, A. D., & Burnett, C. A. (2016). Preparing students for middle school through after-school stem activities. Journal of Science Education & Technology, 25, 1-9.

[2] Mcdonald, C. V. (2016). Stem education: a review of the contribution of the disciplines of science, technology, engineering and mathematics. Science Education International, 27(4), 530-569.

[3] Terracina, A., Mecella, M., Berta, R., Fabiani, F., & Litardi, D. (2016). Game @ School. Teaching Through Gaming and Mobile-Based Tutoring Systems. Springer International Publishing.

[4] Atwood-Blaine, D., & Huffman, D. (2017). Mobile gaming and student interactions in a science center: the future of gaming in science education. International Journal of Science & Mathematics Education, 15(1), 45-65.

[5] Kiili, K. (2007). Foundation for problem-based gaming. British Journal of Educational Technology, 38(3), 394–404.

[6] Chiang, F. K., Li, F. J., & Jiang, S. H. (2016). An Analysis of the Ideas and Teaching Cases of Novel Engineering Education. Information technology education in primary and secondary schools, 7, 75-78.

[7] Wilson-Lopez, A., & Gregory, S. (2015). Integrating literacy and engineering instruction for young learners. Reading Teacher, 69(1), 25–33.

[8] Bressler, D. M., & Bodzin, A. M. (2016). Investigating Flow Experience and Scientific Practices During a Mobile Serious Educational Game. Journal of Science Education & Technology, 25(5), 795-805.

[9] Wouters, P., Van Nimwegen, C., Van Oostendorp, H., & Van, d. S. E. D. (2013). A meta-analysis of the cognitive and motivational effects of serious games. Journal of Educational Psychology, 105(2), 249-265.

[10] Law, V., & Chen, C. H. (2016). Promoting science learning in game-based learning with question prompts and feedback. Computers & Education, 103, 134-143.

[11] Kiili, K. (2005). Digital game-based learning: towards an experiential gaming model. Internet & Higher Education, 8(1), 13-24.

[12] Shang, J. J., Xiang, H. M., & Jia, N. (2014). International education game empirical research review: 2008 -- 2012. E-education Research, 1, 71-78

[13] Davis, F. D. (1989). Perceived usefulness, perceived ease of use, and user acceptance of information technology. Mis Quarterly, 13(3), 319-340.

[14] Csikszentmihalyi, M. (1997). Finding flow: The psychology of engagement with everyday life. New York: Basic Books

[15] Vijayasarathy L R. Predicting consumer intentions to use on-line shopping: the case for an augmented technology acceptance model[J]. Information & Management, 2004, 41(6):747-762.

AUTHORS

Yaoxian Zhuang is a graduate student in the Department of Educational Technology, School of Education, Shanghai Normal University, China, CO 200000, CHINA .

Liyan Wang is with the Department of Educational Technology, School of Education, Shanghai Normal University, China, CO 200000, CHINA .

Feng-kuang Chiang is a professor in the Department of Educational Technology at Shanghai Normal University, China. His research focused on STEM education, learning space and integration of information technology and curriculum(e-mail: fkchiang@shnu.edu.cn).

AUTHOR INDEX